FINALLY HOME

Ethel Waters Finally Home

by Juliann DeKorte

Fleming H. Revell Company
Old Tappan, New Jersey

Library of Congress Cataloging in Publication Data

DeKorte, Juliann.
    Finally home.

    At head of title: Ethel Waters.
    1. Waters, Ethel, 1900-1977. 2. Singers—United States—Biography. I. Title.
ML420.W24D4   783.7'092'4 [B]   78-5697
ISBN 0-8007-0934-9

TO my family—
My husband, Paul
Our children: Stephen, Suzanne, and Alicia
My mother, Bessie DeBruin
In memory of my father, Jacob DeBruin, Jr.

Contents

Preface

As we pass through life, some years stand out as being special, unique, remembered longer than all the others. The year 1977 was such a year for me. It was a difficult year—one of struggle, of watching a loved one suffer, and thus suffering along. Yet the memory of that year is warm and beautiful.

If we are fortunate in life, we cross paths with a few people who are special, who permanently affect our lives, even our very souls. They change us, and we feel a certain kinship with them that separates them from the rest of humanity. Ethel Waters was such a person to me. Her quality of life enriched mine, and simply by being herself, she influenced me deeply.

This is not a book on grief. I did not grieve for her, and I know of no one close to her who did. Having witnessed her suffering and her intense desire to go to her heavenly home, grieving would have been mockery. Yet her bed is empty, the room looms silently, and no one smiles out in love or teases in laughter as I pass by in my daily tasks. I miss that terribly.

I want to give all the praise and honor for this story to the only One deserving it—the Lord Jesus Christ. Our family is not an unusual one. Out of all the thousands who knew Ethel Waters, for a short period of time the Lord chose to use us for this unique ministry. He is never dependent on any one individual to do His work—if we weren't available, He would have used someone else. The only difference is that we would have missed out on the blessing. I'm thankful that He allowed us to serve Him in this way.

Ethel Waters loved the songs she was famous for singing. She lived the lyrics in her personal life, and each one was special in a unique way. It would have been difficult for me to tell her story without them, for they reveal her innermost thoughts and feelings. The lyrics written at the beginning of each chapter are selected from those she regularly used as a gospel singer.

I praise God for my wonderful family, which shared every bit of the load with me. I thank Paul for his constant loving encouragement and support, and our children for their patience and continuous interest.

I am thankful for my dear mother, who provided a loving Christian home for me, teaching me early of Jesus' love. She supports me daily with her prayers, making me believe I can do anything, with the Lord's help. Also I am grateful for the long hours she spent correcting and typing the final manuscript.

I must mention my appreciation to my friends Pat Dempsey, Kay DeVries, and Pat Holt for their enthusiasm; to Margaret Johnson, who helped me get started in the right direction; and a special thank you to Eleanore Schellenberger, who on many occasions helped to care for Mom Waters.

I want to express my admiration for Richard Friedman, M.D., who respected his patient's wishes and allowed her to die in the manner and place she desired.

And above all, my deepest appreciation to Ethel Waters—"Mom"—for generously sharing her life and death with me.

FINALLY HOME

1

Stand by Me

When I'm growing old and feeble,
Stand by me.
When I'm growing old and feeble,
Stand by me.
When my life becomes a burden,
And I'm nearing chilly Jordan,
Oh Thou Lily of the Valley,
Stand by me.

C. A. TINDLEY

The huge clock on the wall pointed to 11:00 P.M. as I entered that all-too-familiar room on the night of August 31, 1977. Something in the air made me stop short just inside the door. I stood silently, surveying the drama before me as if viewing a still-life painting.

It was a large room, appearing gloomy and foreboding, with dark wood paneling covering the walls. The floor was parquet, with green, heavy antique area rugs adding much-needed warmth. Furniture crammed into every inch of available space gave the room a cluttered look.

Three chairs were standing empty, waiting for the visitors who were always expected, but seldom came. Over the chairs were draped handmade knitted afghans collected as presents over the years. Various chests and shelves lined the walls, covered with trophies, knickknacks, and artificial-flower arrangements—all battered and timeworn, all too precious to discard.

On every available wall space were scattered plaques, awards, and pictures smiling down as though in silent mockery of happier days. A stereo stood still in the far corner. One TV and two radios were playing soft melodious music, but no one was listening.

Signs of sickness were scattered about the room. Three oxygen tanks stood in a row. The over-bed table was littered with water pitchers, glasses, and straws. A wheelchair and commode were situated off to one side, adding to the discord. Among all the paraphernalia stood a hospital bed, with trapeze apparatus swinging above and electrical equipment below. In the bed rested a frail woman of eighty. She lay motionless, her eyes closed.

As often as I had stood in this room, I knew that tonight was different. Something about the woman wasn't the same, and in that instant I realized with a sinking heart what it was.

The one who occupied this bed had been exuberant, joyful, always full of zestful living, her eyes twinkling, her mind sharp, her humor quick. Words could fall from her lips soothingly or cutting sharply, like a fine-bladed knife. She sensed, before anyone could tell her, what was happening worldwide as well as in our home. She kept track of our children and their activities with wide-eyed interest. She was a proud lady, primping her hair until it stood shining and white about her face.

But now, on this cool California summer night, she was unaware of her wrinkled bedcovers or her disheveled hair. She didn't even know that I stood watching her. Her only movement was a constant struggle to take in one more breath.

Instinctively, I knew that what I had anticipated for months was imminent. Sometimes, for her sake, I had welcomed it, but now, standing face-to-face with the stark reality, I felt a chill causing quick tears to surface. The woman was dying.

I tiptoed to her side and leaned close to her ashen face. How I loved her! "Mom," I whispered softly. There was no reply. The seconds ticked by on the relentless clock. Once more I called, this time more urgently, my lips close to her ear. "Mom, Mom, can you hear me?"

The response was slight—just a facial expression, then the movement of her face toward mine. The answer came so softly I could barely make out the words: "Yes, angel."

I sighed in relief. "It's eleven o'clock. I'm going to get you ready for sleep now."

The usual quip that followed was absent tonight. Silence was my only reply.

As a registered nurse, I had learned my profession well through hours of caring for patients in the hospital. Now it seemed as though I were caring for a stranger, so intent was I on my medical evaluation. The vital signs were basically unchanged, though I noted the heartbeat had slowed slightly. Blood pressure was normal, breathing was slow and labored, but regular. My patient was very lethargic but could be awakened and was oriented. Her body extremities were cold and edematous. Her condition was poor but, for the present, stable.

"Are you in pain, Mom?" I asked, knowing the answer.

"Yes. My left leg," came the labored reply.

I fixed an injection of pain-killing medicine. "You need something to ease the pain and help you rest. I'm going to give you a shot now," I hesitantly said as I approached the bed. I hurriedly administered the medication before I'd receive the expected retort from my patient. I felt my heart pounding as I stood in silence and realized the change in her. For the first time in the nine months I had cared for her, there was no refusal, or even reluctance, to take medication.

Finally I was satisfied I had done everything I could to make my special patient as comfortable as possible. As I turned from checking the oxygen supply I said, "Tonight I'm going to stay in the room with you. When you need me, just say my name, and I'll hear you."

Once again, no argument. Not the usual, "Don't worry, sweetheart, I'll be all right. You go on upstairs." Instead only the desperate nodding of her head came in agreement. She was too weak to answer verbally.

Then the end of our routine, a kiss on the familiar forehead and the words, "Good-night, sweet Mom. Sleep good." I stood back to accept the loving words that always came as a reply, but they did not come. My only reply was the sound of a lonely cricket on the porch outside the open window.

I walked across the room and prepared the reclining

chair with blankets and pillow to use as my bed. Usually I slept on the couch in the adjoining living room, but tonight I knew my patient did not have the strength to ring the buzzer that hung within her reach. I settled down, too weary to care that I could not stretch out fully.

As had been my practice since childhood, I paused to pray before dropping off to sleep. I closed my eyes, feeling the Lord's presence in the room. I talked to Him as the dear Friend and Helper I desperately needed at that moment.

"Oh, Father, I'm tired, and Mom is suffering so. I know we've asked You many times before to release her from her worn-out body and take her home to be with You. This is what she wants—this is what we all want for her. For some reason You have not seen fit to do this. It seems tonight the time is coming near when You will take her. Give us both the peace and comfort only You can give. Help us through the long night ahead. In the name of my Saviour Jesus Christ. Amen."

I opened my eyes, glanced at my precious patient once more, then closed my eyes to welcome the sleepiness overtaking me. But—ten minutes, twenty minutes, thirty minutes later—and sleep did not come. The hiss of the oxygen leaving the tank was too loud. The smell of disinfectant was too strong. The picture in my mind of the lady in bed was too vivid. My eyes flipped open. Sleep was out of the question!

Who was this lady? Why did she belong to our family when she was not a relative? What was I doing, caring for her?

It was obvious from glancing over the pictures that

lined the walls that this was someone who had been a celebrity. She had had famous people, even presidents, for friends. I had never met a president. It was easy to see she had been very rich at one time. I had never been rich. By looking at the picture of her as a child, one could see she was once surrounded by poverty. I had never been poor. Her race was Negro—I was Caucasian. She was elderly—I was still a young woman.

What did we have in common? Where did it all begin? How did a naive young mother like me, raised in middle-class America, protected by loving Christian parents, come to have someone living with me who had come from such depths and risen to such heights?

I remembered the time four weeks before, after her last hospitalization, when Dr. Friedman said, "Julie, Mom wants to go home. There's nothing more we can do. It's only a matter of time. It could be days or it could be months. Now the question is, Are you up to taking her home again? I know you have a family to care for, and you certainly have gone beyond the call of duty. Tell me, how does your husband feel about your spending all this time taking care of her?"

I couldn't help but chuckle at his question. "My husband? Don't worry about him. He loves her, too. In fact, I came to know her through my husband . . . ."

I could still picture that cold winter day, so many years before. I was a nineteen-year-old nursing student in Michigan, miserable because the one I loved—and would soon marry—had left and gone to California to pursue a career in music. The announcement in the dormitory that the mail had arrived brought a welcome relief to the long hours of study.

I waited impatiently, like everyone else, while the letters were placed in the mailboxes. Finally one was slipped into mine. My hand fumbled with the combination, and at last my fingers ripped open the envelope with the beloved familiar writing. Without taking time to retreat to the quiet of my room, I began to devour each word, completely oblivious to others moving about me in the same state of mind.

"Honey . . ." it began. My eyes raced on as if it had been two years, instead of two days, since I had received such a letter.

It continued: "It is early morning, and I couldn't wait to tell you! Last night I met someone and . . . I fell in love!"

What? My mind exploded with a thousand questions at once. I didn't take time to explore any of them, however, as my eyes continued to rush ahead.

"I hope you don't mind, dear. I know when you meet her, you'll love her too. She is anxious to meet you. Dick and I are going to be singing with her in concerts and church programs. She's sixty-five years old, and the sweetest, most lovable person you'll ever know. Her name is Ethel Waters."

2

The Joy of Giving

I'm going to live
The way He wants me to live,
I'm going to give
Until there's just no more to give,
I'm going to love, love
'Til there's just no more love,
I could never, never outlove the Lord!
GLORIA AND WILLIAM J. GAITHER

I heard my name being whispered from the stillness. Before my mind was fully aware of what was happening, I jumped up and rushed to the bedside. "Yes, Mom. What is it?" I asked anxiously. The high pitch of my voice revealed the trepidation I felt.

Slowly and with great difficulty came a mumbled question in reply: "What time is it?"

I reached out and grasped her hand, stroking it reassuringly while giving myself time to gain control over my voice. "It's just after midnight," I answered, glancing at the clock.

How thrilled she had been on Mother's Day when we all presented her with that big clock. It was a welcome addition to the room, ending the strain of trying to see the small one at the bedside through eyes that could see very little.

"Oh! Children, I love it!" she had squealed, hands clasped and eyes sparkling. We all stood around the bed, beaming with satisfaction, for Ethel Waters was by no means the easiest person in the world for whom to buy a present. The chests of drawers in the room were overflowing with presents from admirers, so when we discovered something useful, we were rightly proud of ourselves.

"Put it straight across the room from me," she had firmly directed, pointing a finger to the exact spot. "Right there on the wall, where I can see it day and night without having to twist my neck. There, that's perfect. Oh, that's nice," she admired as it was positioned in place.

We all stood back and admired the large round clock, agreeing how fantastic it was, as if it were a mink coat or a Rolls Royce!

This night, however, as I looked at it, I didn't see the friend I saw before. It was just an ordinary clock, and the seconds racing by were a constant reminder that time was running out.

"Would you like some water?" I asked, noticing her gaping mouth and parched lips.

She nodded in agreement and struggled for the strength to suck one small sip through the straw I held. Finally, when the difficult feat was accomplished, she lacked the strength to swallow, and her body shook violently in painful choking spasms.

I stood close by, helping in whatever way I could, and gradually the color returned to her lips as her breathing resumed. The episode took its toll, however, sapping the little strength remaining in her body. Without saying a word, she closed her eyes and slipped off into a semiconscious state.

The realization that my special patient had slipped so far that she could no longer swallow struck me with a startling jolt, causing my heart to tear a little more with each of her labored breaths.

My medical evaluation told me that her breathing was more labored than before. One hand searched the pulse on her wrist while the other groped for the oxygen knob, turning the flow up two more liters per minute. Because she could no longer hold her mouth closed, most of the oxygen was not reaching the lungs, where it was desperately needed.

The slow intermittent pressure of the pulse against my fingers gave me a feeling of reassurance that is so welcome and familiar to any nurse who cares for a critical patient. "Oh, thank You, Lord," I silently rejoiced. "Her heart is still strong."

I pulled over a chair and sat down next to the bed, holding the withered hand so dear to me. Why was I holding on? What was I afraid of? Wasn't this what she had prayed and longed for with joyful expectation? Wasn't a full, exciting, rewarding long life enough for anyone?

Yes, of course it was enough. It was more than enough.

How wonderful the Lord was to His dear saint, to allow her to be actively serving Him until the last year of her life. Yes, if my love was genuine, there was nothing more I could wish for Mom than for her to be with her Lord. How wonderful that would be!

The portion of the Bible I read to her a few nights before flashed through my mind. I recalled how the Apostle Paul had said:

> According to my earnest expectation and hope, that I shall not be put to shame in anything, but that with all boldness, Christ shall even now, as always, be exalted in my body, whether by life or by death. For to me, to live is Christ, and to die is gain. But if I am to live on in the flesh, this will mean fruitful labor for me; and I do not know which to choose. But I am hard-pressed from both directions, having the desire to depart and be with Christ, for that is very much better.
>
> Philippians 1:20–23 NAS

"Yes, Jesus, I agree with the Apostle Paul," Mom had exclaimed, looking heavenward as I finished. "Please let me come home!" Then she submissively added, "If it's Your will!"

People have written volumes about Ethel Waters. She has been quoted and talked about on television, radio, and in private conversations all over the world. She proved herself to be a legend in her own age: an actress, singer, humorist, and entertainer par excellence. Her talent of communication was such that she could bring tears to the eyes of the stalwart by singing just one song.

But I knew a different Ethel Waters—a quiet, private person who shied away from the crowds, parties, and gaiety of the entertainment world. As I looked back on our relationship that night, I realized the profound effect she had on my life.

We were as mother and child from the beginning. Recently we were patient and nurse. But all along, she was instructing me in a different relationship—that of teacher and student. She used the tool of example subtly, skillfully maneuvering without saying a word, so that I was unaware of her intentions. She took her responsibilities seriously, as directed by Scripture:

> Older women likewise are to be reverent in their behavior . . . teaching what is good, that they may encourage the young women to love their husbands, to love their children, to be sensible, pure, workers at home . . . that the word of God may not be dishonored.
>
> Titus 2:3–5 NAS

One of the first lessons Ethel Waters taught me was the joy of giving. She showed me how to share myself and my possessions with others, to give away what I possess materially and spiritually.

Ethel Waters came into my life when I was a timid young woman groping for an identity. I was a new bride, freshly graduated from nurses' training, working at my first job with strange people in unfamiliar surroundings. With her intuitive sense, she immediately took me under her wings, mothering and protecting me.

"Don't worry about her while Mom's here," she once laughingly said to my parents while they were visiting. "I'll watch out after her!"

Quickly sizing me up as green, she told me over and over, much to my irritation, "Darlin', you just don't know what it's like out there. [She was speaking of the world.] It's rough!" I often felt intimidated when she spoke proudly of a friend or acquaintance and proclaimed, "Now, *they* know what it's like to come up from the bottom. *They've* had it rough!"

That night I thought how our roles had changed over the past few months. How helpless she was now, dependent on me for meeting her every physical need. But it had not always been that way. She had always been the leader, but over the past few months she had been forced to depend on others for her very existence.

One of the first things we got settled in our relationship was what we were to call her. It was definitely to be "Mom." I'll never forget the first time I slipped and called her Ethel by mistake. I got a look that would chill anyone, and from then on, I always remembered!

Ethel Waters never bore any children of her own, so to compensate for this, she adopted any and every person she could. "Just call me Mom," she would instruct friends, loved ones, and even strangers. She loved to be called Mom.

My husband, Paul, and his friend Dick Bolks had been adopted by Mom the year before I arrived in California. Dick was an accomplished pianist, and Paul a vocal soloist. Together they also made a vocal duet team. At the time we began working together, Ethel Waters had just rededicated her life to the Lord. She was extremely overweight, making it difficult for her to walk, sing, or speak for any length of time. In spite of her handicap, the Lord had an exciting new career ahead for His devoted servant, leading her into a ministry of sacred concerts that took her all over the country. She trusted Him to provide the strength she needed for His work.

Dick Bolks was accompanying her at these concerts, and when Paul went along with them one evening, she suddenly said on the way home, "Why don't you two children of mine just give ol' Mom a rest and do some singing in the middle of my concerts?"

They eagerly seized the opportunity. After opening the concert, Mom would present about twenty minutes of message in word and song. Then, completely breathless, she would sit and rest while "her boys" filled in with ten or fifteen minutes of solos and duets. When she felt rested enough to conclude the program with another twenty minutes, she would signal them with her eyes and they would conclude their part of the concert.

We traveled together for a few years, joyfully serving the Lord, until our first two children came along, forcing us to settle down a bit. During that time we had the opportunity of helping a little in Mom's ministry, and she in turn gave us encouragement, love, and the security of belonging to someone in a strange big city.

Along with giving us herself, she loved to lavish us with material things, paying us far beyond what we earned for working with her. Delight always registered on her jolly face when she had the pleasure of helping us financially.

I saw that same childish look of delight over and over again, since she loved to lavish gifts on people who crossed her path. "They are sent into my life for a purpose," she'd proudly instruct us. "The Lord tells me to help."

In those early years of our marriage, when Mom often came for dinner, she surveyed our house closely. When she saw a need, she tried her best to supply it. We, of course, were only two names on a long, long list of people, young and old, who benefited from knowing her. If there was a need, she wouldn't rest until it was filled, even if she had to do without to provide it. Anyone spending time with her came away laden with spiritual and material gifts—it was inevitable.

I suppose to those looking on, her bank account was meager. A few thousand dollars saved from a lifetime isn't much, but she didn't believe in purchasing stocks or building up interest in a bank. She invested in lives.

How could anyone become wealthy while raising a number of youngsters, even though she had none of her own? How could she build a huge bank account when all through her life she supported several other people? Only the Lord knows the sacrifices she made in order to give to others.

My eyes searched around the room as I wondered where now were all those beautiful possessions, so fondly remembered. Only a small percentage of what she used to have was moved here from her apartment.

Most were gladly given to loved ones who cherished them because of their special owner.

My thoughts jumped to a bright spring day a few months before. The mail had arrived, and with anticipation of the joy it would bring her, I took her mail to her room. Her spirits were as light as the warm breeze coming in the open window.

"Well, what do we have today, sweetheart?" she asked with interest.

"Let's see," I mumbled as I shuffled through the envelopes. "There's a letter from your lawyer and some fan mail and two bills."

"Forget the bills and leave the fan mail until later. Let's hear the letter from the lawyer."

I ripped open the envelope and prepared to read the enclosed letter to her, since her poor eyesight made it impossible for her to read. "Dear Paul and Julie," it began. I looked at her questioningly.

She nodded, with a twinkle in her eye. "Go on," she ordered briskly.

"Because of my love for you, I am herewith giving you my personal belongings and furniture moved here from my apartment . . . ."

"Oh, Mom, I can't read this," I cried. "Please. Don't make me."

"Now how am I supposed to know whether it's correct if you don't read it?" Her voice disclosed irritation. "Go ahead. Read it—all of it," she ordered.

I reluctantly obeyed and finished the letter. "Mom," I said when I finished, "I don't know what to say. You keep your things. You may need them."

"Now, baby," she replied, "you know that's not true. When I leave this house I don't intend to take a thing with me, 'cause where I'm going, I won't be needing anything. Everything has been provided. I want someone to have the few nice things I have left—someone who will appreciate them. And that's you. So we won't discuss it anymore. It's all settled," she said with stubborn finality. "Now I can forget about it and rest, knowing that's been taken care of!"

When someone came to visit her, she delighted in giving them something to take away with them. She often spent the entire visit trying to figure out what would be the best gift for a visitor. Other times she delighted in saving a wrapped present for months—even a year—relishing the suspense of wondering what was inside.

While she was a patient in the hospital, a visitor would proudly present Mom with a plant or an arrangement of flowers, only to have her send it home with her next visitor! It did no good to try to change her mind once it was made up. Ethel Waters had been on her own too long to be told what to do.

Only once do I recall her giving herself a present. It was just after she came to live with us, and we were all concerned because her eyesight had regressed greatly during the time in the hospital. She could no longer see the small television screen she owned, which was her main source of entertainment. She asked Paul to check on what was available with a larger screen and a remote-control unit. He found a nice big one with a zoom feature that could bring the picture even closer.

She wanted that television very badly, but the cost was

quite high. Finally, after days of thinking and talking to
the Lord about it, she called Paul into her room.

"You know, son," she said, "all my life I've given to
others and never kept a lot for myself. I don't think it's
wrong if just this once I get something I don't particu-
larly need, but would enjoy—just for myself."

That television set brought her hours of companion-
ship and enjoyment, enabling her to laugh and cry with
her friends and acquaintances who performed on it from
day to day. It helped in its small way to ease her pain and
fill some of the hours of each day with the mental stimulation that she needed to keep sharp and aware of what
was going on outside the little world of her room. It was
worth every penny!

The pattern of giving continued throughout Mom's
lifetime—a habit that came from deep within the soul of
one who once had nothing and was now grateful to be
able to share.

> . . . he who sows sparingly shall also reap spar-
> ingly; and he who sows bountifully shall also reap
> bountifully.
>
> 2 Corinthians 9:6 NAS

3

The Blessings of Hospitality

I am a poor pilgrim of sorrow,
I'm tossed in this wide world alone,
No hope have I for tomorrow,
I've started to make heaven my home!
Sometimes I am tossed an' driven, Lord,
Sometimes I don't know where to roam,
I heard of a city called heaven,
I've started to make it my home.
                    TRADITIONAL SPIRITUAL

The hushed quiet of the night was abruptly broken by the loud roar of a car passing on the street. The noise caused my head to jerk up as I was beginning to nod with sleepiness.

"Where in the world is someone going in such a hurry at this time of night?" I wondered. How incredible that someone should pass so close and yet be completely unaware of the drama going on in the house shrouded in seemingly peaceful silence. I wondered how many times I had unknowingly passed by a battle between life and death and in my ignorance offered no help.

I gingerly reached out to close the window, but despite my caution, it gave out an irritatingly high-pitched squeak. I could hear the bedcovers moving, and without turning around, I knew the noise had aroused my patient.

"Julie," she called weakly.

"Yes, Mom? I'm here," I replied, annoyed at myself for disturbing her rest. "Did you want something?"

"No, I just wanted to hear your voice. It helps me," came the raspy reply.

"I won't leave. I'll stay right here," I said, trying to reassure her that she was not alone in the fight to live. I watched the covers move up and down with the regular rhythm of her breathing. The respirations were becoming more rapid—something that usually happens as the body tries to compensate for the extra oxygen it needs to remain functioning.

"I can sense you're here, even though I can't see you," she said between gasps. Her eyes did not open.

"Try to get some rest, Mom. Your body needs it." I might as well have talked to myself, because the regular groaning resumed, signaling that my patient had once again drifted off.

I slowly walked over and eased down into the reclining chair, pulling the welcome warmth of the blanket tightly up around my neck. Surely this time I would be able to sleep. With my eyes closed, I was suddenly aware of all the noises coming in from the dark night, and it encouraged me to know that others were in some way sharing my vigil.

Yes, life goes on. All nature seems indifferent to the fact that someone is in her final wrestling match. Here in this room my loved one was dying, but I knew that across town, in the hospital I was so familiar with, some other woman would be in travail with the agony of birth. A new life, a new beginning. What a vicious circle we are thrust into at birth. This is a circle God never intended when He created man, but in His omniscience He knew it would come to be. We are born to die, although God created us to live.

How well I remembered the excitement we all felt at the birth of our first child. Mom Waters was just as excited as anyone, and I remembered the warmth of pride we felt as we placed him for the first time in those big lovable arms.

"Children always settle down and are quiet when they are in my arms," she informed us. "I don't know what it is they sense about me, but it has always been true."

And so it was. Our little one was content, relishing the security of snuggling in those soft arms that loved to hold him. Her face beamed down, lips puckered in the frivolous babblings of baby talk—a language he seemed to understand, since he cooed back seriously in answer.

We traveled with the baby for a short time at Mom's insistence. "Are Julie and my baby coming this Saturday?" she would ask Paul. No one could take care of that baby like she could!

One night she was holding Stephen while being interviewed by a newspaper reporter. Being interviewed wasn't Ethel Waters' favorite way to spend a half hour, to put it mildly! During this particular interview, she sat quietly backstage in a high-school auditorium and smiled at the month-old baby in her arms, fondling and talking to him while the frustrated reporter tried to get her attention.

"I only intend to please the Saviour. That's the main objective of my life," she emphatically pronounced. Then she proceeded to give him a fast overview of her fifty years in show business.

"I don't like to talk about the past. It's the present that concerns me, and what people think about my Lord," she continued, trying to keep the conversation centered on her Saviour. She had become an expert at turning every question back to the only subject worth talking about, in her opinion.

The baby in her arms awoke and began to fuss. With a hearty laugh, Mom looked at me and said, "I think it's about that time, Mommie!" Then turning to the reporter, she said with a sly chuckle, "This is where I cut out!"

I took our son from her and went back to one of the dressing rooms to change and feed him. When I reappeared several minutes later, she was still occupied with the reporter.

"Yes, I've had it tough," I heard her say. "But when you compare our lives with the way they treated Christ, we're getting off easy!"

Her eyes caught sight of me approaching and they lit up as she held her hands out, indicating she was ready to resume her role as grandmother. With the same chuckle, she turned to the reporter and said, "Excuse me, but this is where I cut in again!"

The baby settled down with a sigh, and Mom eagerly resumed her cooing and cuddling. The poor reporter finally decided that he was no match for the baby and politely excused himself. The baby remained completely satisfied in Mom's lap until it was time for her to go onstage.

One thing I found out right away about Ethel Waters was that it was impossible to win on a point in which I differed in opinion from her. She had been on her own, practically since birth, and was used to being completely independent and having her own way. She knew best—and that was that!

Mom had several notions about taking care of babies—ideas that we tended to label "old wives' tales" in nurses' training. She believed strongly that even on a ninety-degree day, a baby's feet should be covered, or else there was danger he would catch a cold. Shortly I realized that the whole thing wasn't worth seeing her uncomfortable about those "cold little toes," so when we were around Mom, our baby wore bootees!

As our family grew, we felt the Lord leading Paul to accept a position on the music staff at one of the large churches in Los Angeles. About the same time, Mom's health declined, and she had to curtail the amount of time she was actively ministering, saving her strength for the major Billy Graham Crusades. We realized reluctantly that our time of traveling together had come to a close.

As I mulled over those years, I thought of the many fond memories we had and of the many lessons we learned through the experience. We would be forever grateful to Ethel Waters for helping us so much in the beginning of our married life.

During the next ten years we saw Mom relatively little. We kept in touch by telephone, but it was difficult for her to come to our home for dinner. When we visited her, we kept the visit short—one cuddly baby was one thing, but three active children were something else!

Each Thanksgiving and Christmas I would cook an extra turkey with all the trimmings, plus homemade soup and other goodies to save for future meals, and take it to her ahead of time. She loved home cooking so much, and since she had to maintain a rigid diet most of the time, those meals were greatly looked forward to.

We asked Mom several times to come and make her home with us whenever living alone proved difficult for her. But it was so important for her to maintain her independence, and the Lord always prevented it for one reason or another. He knew that the time was coming when He would bring us together again for a special time in Ethel Waters' life.

On Christmas, 1975, Mom confided to me that she had been hemorrhaging for some time. My reaction was one of alarm. "Please make an appointment and see your doctor at once," I urged her. "Be very specific and honest about the whole situation."

What followed was unfortunately what frequently happens when someone has a severe medical problem. She procrastinated. The time was never convenient; she was too busy; and besides, she had just been in the hospital to have her eyes operated on, and it had not been a pleasant experience. She wasn't about to go back!

By that following summer, she was very weak from loss of blood, and so she reluctantly admitted herself to a hospital. The diagnosis wasn't a surprise to any who knew the warning symptoms—cancer of the uterus.

I only managed to make the long trip to see her in the hospital once. The children's schedule made the trip very difficult, and the radiation treatments given to Mom caused her to be very weak, so she did not want to see anyone. I came away from that one visit alarmed and depressed at the amount of pain she was enduring and at her general regressed physical condition.

On Thanksgiving Day, 1976, we stopped by to see her on our way to the mountains, but we were not greeted by our usual exuberant friend. She was glad to see us, but out of her mouth came surprising words: "Oh, children, what's going to become of me? My treatments here are finished, and soon I know they'll ask me to leave. I can't go back to my apartment—I'm too weak to even stand up!"

Paul replied calmly, "You know you always have a place with us. Why don't you come out and stay at our home? We have a room downstairs you'd love, and it has an adjoining bath."

"That's right, Mom," I chimed in. "Why don't you come and stay with us? I'll quit my part-time job and stay home and take care of you. I'd love to do that!"

Because I was aware of how much her own apartment meant to her, I quickly added, "It doesn't have to be for a long time. Just for a few weeks, until you get on your feet. Then you can go back home again." It was so important to her to be independent and on her own, but deep down inside, I wondered whether this sweet, lovable woman would ever be able to live by herself again.

We kept our visit short and didn't discuss the situation any further, but I could see the wheels turning, and I knew we left her with something constructive to think about and discuss with her Lord.

A few weeks later I had occasion to go near the hospital again, and I decided to stop in and see Mom. I opened the door on the same pathetic scene. She was lying on her side in the darkened hospital room. The drapes were tightly shut and the air stagnant. This time she looked at me with anxious, hopeful eyes and blurted out, "Oh, Julie, did you mean what you said to me before?"

"Of course we meant it, Mom," I assured her. "Christmas is coming, you know. Wouldn't it be nice to leave the hospital and be with us for the holidays? Can't you smell the cookies baking now?"

She nodded her head slowly, but it was a nod filled with apprehension. She had been in that hospital room for three months, only leaving it on a stretcher to go down the hall for radiation treatments. Since she had never been to our new home, she faced going to an unknown situation. I continued to reassure her, and we agreed to leave it all in the Lord's hands. If it was His will, it would most certainly all work out.

Before I left she said, "I've been talking to the Lord about it all the time since you were here before, and He keeps telling me, 'Go to Paul and Julie's!'"

Knowing the close relationship Ethel Waters had with

her Saviour, I felt a renewed commitment that this was ordained from above. Before leaving, I tore a piece of paper off a pad on the bedside table and wrote our telephone number on it.

"There. See, Mom? I've written our telephone number on this paper," I cheerfully said, holding the paper close to her dim eyes. "Now when someone tells you it's time for you to leave, you just have a nurse call, and we'll be out here to get you."

The tenseness began to drain out of her face as she looked heavenward and uttered her familiar, "Thank You, Jesus. It's all up to You now."

I had called ahead and made an appointment with one of Mom's doctors, so I immediately left for his office. It was a stiff, cold room, and I was filled with apprehension as I greeted the cordial physician. Explaining the situation to him—who I was and what we were thinking of doing—I asked him to level with me regarding her condition, prognosis, and when she would be ready to leave.

"First of all, Mrs. DeKorte," he said, "I want you to realize what an awesome responsibility you are taking on." He looked at me sternly. "A young mother like yourself just doesn't realize the demands of caring for an invalid in a home. I'm not worried about your family, but I am worried about you. You know," he continued as I squirmed in my seat, "you can't walk away from this patient like you can in a hospital. She'll be there to take care of twenty-four hours a day!"

I wiggled down further in the seat and swallowed hard. It was frightening to hear someone verbalize all the thoughts already in my mind.

Mercilessly he continued, "There will be times when she will need you, and your children will need you at the same time. Will she understand? She doesn't realize the demands of a home. I know what I'm talking about—we tried it once in our home, and it didn't work." I thought he was finished, but he quickly added, "Might I say that, while we all love her, she has been a very difficult patient to handle."

He proceeded to give me the details of her treatment and informed me that the prognosis was good for the present, since the tumor had remarkably decreased in size. As for when she should leave, he said the sooner the better. She had been in the hospital for so long that she needed the mental stimulation of a different environment.

We agreed that he would tell her that, in order to get her strength back faster, she should plan to leave no later than the following week. I left the room, thanking the doctor, telling him that the Lord had brought this all about and that I was trusting Him to work out the problems.

Soon I was on my way home, driving in the welcome solitude of my automobile. I had a good long time to sort things out in my mind on the trip. What if she was unhappy at our house? I couldn't expect the children to walk around the house as if on eggshells! Would they resent her as an intruder? What if she were so demanding I couldn't please her?

What about all my responsibilities at church, school, and work? Would people understand when I gave everything up? The questions pounded my mind, until I finally said aloud, "Lord, I just trust You! I didn't seek this, and so I'm taking it from You. You take complete charge and work out every detail!"

I didn't realize it that day as I drove along, but the Lord, with the help of Ethel Waters, was going to teach me another valuable lesson about the Christian life—the immeasurable blessing of hospitality.

The first thing we had to take care of was how we were going to handle this whole thing with our children. Christmas was coming, and they would be home for two weeks. Life around the house would drastically change. The Christmas season is always busy, but this year it would be more hectic than ever.

After dinner that night we explained to the children that Grandma Waters was coming to live with us for a while. We mentioned how very sick she was and how painful her condition was and that she needed us all to help her and make her happy.

Since we firmly believe that God's Word contains the answer for anything that comes our way, we naturally read the passage on hospitality found in Matthew 25:

Then the King will say to those on His right, "Come you who are blessed of My Father, inherit the kingdom prepared for you from the foundation of the world. For I was hungry, and you gave Me something to eat; I was thirsty, and you gave Me drink; I was a stranger, and you invited Me in; naked and you clothed Me; I was sick, and you visited Me; I was in prison, and you came to Me." Then the righteous will answer Him, saying, "Lord, when did we

see You hungry, and feed You, or thirsty, and give
You drink? And when did we see You a stranger, and
invite You in, or naked and clothe You? And when
did we see You sick, or in prison, and come to You?"
And the King will answer and say to them, "Truly I
say to you, to the extent that you did it to one of
these brothers of Mine, even the least of them, you
did it to Me."

                                    Matthew 25:34–40 NAS

We waited while Paul turned to Mark and continued:

For whoever gives you a cup of water to drink because of your name as followers of Christ, truly I say
to you, he shall not lose his reward.

                                    Mark 9:41 NAS

"Now, children," he began, "we've already mentioned that Grandma Waters is coming here to live, and
your mother is going to take care of her. We've just read
that when we take care of the needs of one of God's
children, then God the Father looks on that act as if we
were doing it for His Son, Jesus Christ. So that's how
we're going to look at it—we are going to be caring for
Jesus in our home."

We all agreed we had been given an exciting opportunity. "Now we're all going to have to pitch in and help,"
Paul instructed. "Maybe Mommie can't drive the bas-
ketball team, or sew the dress you want, or help with
homework quite as much. And we'll expect more help

around the house. But that's nothing," he exclaimed, "because we're doing it for Jesus, and that's such a privilege!"

In all the long months that we had a bedridden invalid in our home, the children never showed even the slightest resentment. I knew only too well that they were normal children—they had always done their share of grumbling, complaining, and balking at many of the things they were told to do. Only the Lord could have given them such a positive attitude!

Hospitality is something God expects all Christians to give. Yet how many of us actually do put ourselves out for another? We know that God had promised blessing and strength for everything He directs, and to be hospitable is one of those things He wants for us.

No, it wasn't always easy. It's never easy seeing a loved one in constant pain. It wasn't always convenient. Regularly one of the children could be found outside the door of Mom's room, waiting for me to appear and answer a question. Yes, there was pressure—days of running errands and shopping in a frantic hurry because there was a schedule to keep. Sometimes I felt misunderstood, sometimes unappreciated.

There in Mom's room, as I watched and waited with her, I thought of all the well-meaning people who said, "Oh, how nice of you to take her into your home." I remembered how uncomfortable and uneasy hearing that made me feel. I'd rather have heard, "How wonderful that God has chosen you to take care of His child!" We never felt we were the givers, because she gave us so much more than we could ever give to her. *We* were the blessed!

Exciting? Oh, yes, it's exciting to serve the Lord when no one sees but Him. There is nothing like it. Rewarding? Certainly it is rewarding to help ease the pain of someone and hear, "Thanks, sweetheart, it's so much better." Worthwhile? Absolutely worthwhile—to see your children learn a practical lesson in sharing and watch them gain compassion for the elderly, becoming just a little less self-centered in our affluent, materialistic society.

Hospitality. The blessings are numerous and the rewards beyond compare. Those and other pleasant thoughts about the times we spent together enveloped me like the warm blanket, and I floated off into a soft, peaceful dreamland.

As a child, Ethel grew up in the slums of Chester, Pennsylvania. Her early life was surrounded by poverty. When she became wealthy, she gave of her money freely, always remembering those hard years.

That brilliant smile was always a part of Ethel Waters' appeal. At fourteen she began singing in nightclubs, but she ended her performing career as a part of the Billy Graham Crusade.

Ethel Waters singing one of her hits, "Heat Wave," in *As Thousands Cheer*.

Although Ethel Waters was often in the public spotlight, she was a very private person who avoided interviews and publicity. Eleanor Roosevelt was a personal friend.

Ethel Waters (left), Eddie Rochester, and Lena Horne in a scene from *Cabin in the Sky*, a part of Ethel's second career as a dramatic actress. (*Photograph by United Press International.*)

Ethel's expressive face shows a pensive mood.

Many stars appeared with Ethel Waters. Here she appears with Count Basie in the movie *Stage Door Canteen*. (*Photograph by United Press International.*) *Below:* Ethel Waters enjoying a story told by composer Harold Arlen. Although her career was hailed as being long and brilliant, few people realized that it was also fraught with loneliness. (*Photographs by United Press International.*)

Ethel Waters with Julie Harris and Brandon de Wilde in a scene from her best-known role as Bernice in *Member of the Wedding*. (*Photograph by United Press International.*)

4

A Unique Individual

I'm a pilgrim and a stranger,
That's seeking a home
My Lord has prepared for me.
Now all to Him I surrender,
For now I can see;
He is the answer to all that I need!
TRADITIONAL SPIRITUAL

A loud, lingering groan pierced the stupor of my light sleep. I looked over at the shuddering form of the dear lady lying in the bed. Her eyes were open and glassy, staring at the ceiling while she endured some sharp pain that had seized her body with wicked suddenness.

Once again I jumped up and hurried over to her, reaching out to stroke her arm gently. "I'm here, Mom, if there's anything you want," I said softly.

I watched as the pain mercifully released its grip and the furrowed lines on her face softened a little. Ever so slowly her head moved, and she squinted to see me.

"Why are you upset, honey?" she asked.

"Oh, I'm just concerned about you, and it makes me

sad to see you so uncomfortable," I replied.

I learned a long time ago never to try to pretend around Ethel Waters. It was an impossibility. Everyone who was close to her knew the same thing—we had all felt and seen the effects of her intuitive sense. She was very proud of her ability to discern if someone was being completely honest, or if his motives were totally right in any given situation. After spending a few minutes with a total stranger, she could tell me everything about him. It was not a fortune-telling type of intuition. She was able to sense anyone's basic personality, his goals and motives in life, as well as his sincerity. No one fooled Ethel Waters!

She immediately seemed to relax. If I was only concerned about *her,* then she knew everything was under control. She was at peace. Turning her head away from me, she closed her eyes and drifted off into a restless sleep.

I was surprised at how refreshed I felt after my nap. "Only two-forty-five," I marveled. "I thought I had slept much longer than that." Since I no longer felt sleepy, I decided to sit on the chair by the bed and hold my special patient's hand. Now I could relate to the many relatives who had come to me with anguished faces as their loved ones lay dying.

"Isn't there something I can do?" they would cry out. "I feel so useless!"

I had tried to calm them, not really understanding their frustration until tonight. I encouraged them to stay with their loved one, hold his hand, and reassure him that he was loved. Tonight it was my turn, but I was cast into the dual role of nurse and relative. I would do my best as a nurse, seeing that my patient was as comfortable as possible. And I would stay by her side as a loving relative, letting her know that I cared—that she was not alone.

I wondered how many of my patients in the hospital would have benefited from my sitting down and waiting with them while death came closer? Instead, we nurses are so often not with our patients when they really need us. Rather, we're tied up with a mountain of paperwork or scurrying up and down the halls, trying to do the work of five people. No, tonight I would not fail. Tonight I would stay. Tonight we would wait together.

"How much longer, Lord?" I asked. "How much more does she have to endure?" I remembered other times when I had felt she couldn't live another day, or certainly not another week. But that was weeks, even months, ago—and she had always rallied to face another day. Perhaps this would happen once again. Maybe God's plan for this servant of His was for her to face another day, another week, even another year.

All of a sudden the hiss of the oxygen leaving the tank ceased, and I knew that the tank in use was empty. As I moved to change to a different tank, the new quietness in the room revealed the muffled sound of the radio, inaudible before because of the noise from the life-giving oxygen leaving the tank. Someone was speaking, and I could tell by the intensity of his voice that it was on a subject of utmost importance to him. But tonight, in this room, no one was interested.

I strained to open the tightly sealed valve on the new tank, and eventually it released its grip, allowing the comforting hiss to resume. The radio was forced back into an undecipherable whisper.

The first task to be accomplished the day Mom moved into this room had been to plug in the radio. It had played ever since, as a subtle background to whatever else was taking place in our home. It took a while before we all adjusted to the continuous sound, especially to waking up in the middle of the night to hear someone joyously singing or fervently preaching!

It was an absolutely beautiful day when my mother accompanied me the forty miles to pick Mom up from the hospital. The sky was unusually crystal clear, and the sun reflected brightly off the car as we drove along the freeway.

As I entered the hospital room, I noticed Mom was slightly nervous and agitated with her nurse, fussing about how things should be packed. I speculated that this was brought on by her being apprehensive at leaving the familiarity of the hospital room which had been her home for three months, and at going to a strange situation. I started joking with her about several little things, gradually easing the tension, and she became her cheerful self again.

"I'm so anxious to leave this place," she whispered in my ear when her nurse was occupied across the room. I knew it wasn't because the care hadn't been excellent, but because three months in a hospital is enough for anyone!

"Let me get you a wheelchair, Miss Waters," the nurse offered, noticing the strain etched on her face.

"No!" came the emphatic reply. "I don't want any wheelchair. I'm going to leave this place the same way I came in—walking!"

And so she did. It was an agonizingly slow parade, consisting of Mom Waters, the nurse, a young resident, and myself. But with the Lord's help, we finally made it out the door and down the sidewalk to the car.

As we drove home that day, I felt again as if the weight of the world was being placed on my shoulders. Satan began working on me, placing doubts in my mind as to whether we had reached the right decision regarding bringing an invalid into our home.

Many times I had seen how the personality of the elderly can change after a lengthy hospitalization. The stress and strain of severe illness, plus being torn away from a familiar home, often cause mental changes that are difficult for relatives to handle. Often the elderly become demanding, obstinate, and even rude. I considered also what living in continuous severe physical pain could do to a person's mental attitude. Frequently it caused depression, moodiness, and discouragement.

Is this what had happened to Mom Waters? Was the woman lying in the backseat of my car the same one whose keen sense of humor once kept us in a constant state of hilarity? What if she demanded more than I could give? Would she still love to eat what I prepared—or would I, like the nurse I had just seen, be unable to please her? What adjustments would we all have to make? How would we manage to get through the busy Christmas season, with all of our previous committments?

Somehow, in my weak state of faith, I felt that I would be able to tell from her reaction to the room and its surroundings whether or not this arrangement would work. I nervously helped her out of the car and inside, sensing that she was as apprehensive as I was about what was to occur.

I will never forget the look on her face as she stood in the doorway, gazing at the room we had so carefully prepared for her. The children had eagerly placed a little Christmas tree in the corner of the room and decorated it with lights, tinsel, and ornaments. This, along with electric candles in the window and a beautiful poinsettia plant on the shelf, gave a festive feeling to the room.

The bedsheets were purposefully chosen a delicate blue, to contrast with the sterile-looking hospital white, and a mellow gold bedspread gave an added glow that made the room look inviting. The drapes were already drawn across the window to protect her weak eyes.

She stood leaning on my arm, and her look was one of absolute joy and tremendous relief. "Oh, thank You, Father! Thank You, Jesus! Thank You, thank You!" She repeated it over and over again, tears of appreciation streaming down her cheeks as her eyes looked heavenward.

Then, looking around the room again, she clasped her hands together with delight and exclaimed, "Oh, children, I love it. I can tell I will feel at home here. This is *my* room now!" Then returning her attention to the One who made it all possible, she sobbed, "Jesus, You knew what I needed. Thank You!"

I joyfully scurried about, getting Mom and all of her belongings settled in their new home. I went about my work rejoicing, but ashamed at how I had dreaded the experience that turned out to be so delightful. However, it was the only reaction I could have expected from myself, knowing the complex personality of the one with whom I was dealing.

I had given up long ago trying to understand Ethel Waters. She was completely unpredictable! I learned quickly to love and respect her with the awe that her very presence demanded, while developing a healthy fear of displeasing her. She could be stern and stubborn—yet gentle, loving, and kind. She could be blunt, unyielding, and strict—yet wise, generous, and forgiving. She even became frustrated at times with her own many-faceted personality. She once admitted, "I'm more comfortable with Ethel Waters, now that she's a Christian. But I don't understand her all the time."

With all the complexities she brought along with her, there were only two vital needs she shared with me that day. "Julie, I desperately need a place where I can have my privacy, but also where I can be around people, life, and action. I'm a loner. I've been a loner all my life, darlin', and I'm tired of it."

I had precipitated that remark by speaking harshly to our youngest for making too much noise when Grandma Waters was so sick. Mom immediately called me into her room, having overheard the remark, a routine that was to be repeated many times in the coming months.

"Please don't tell the children they have to be quiet because I'm here," she scolded. "It's their house, and they have a right to be as noisy as they were before I came." Then she continued to explain, "You see, sweetheart, there's love here! That's what I need. I don't want to be in some room shut off from activity and living. I want to be a part of things!" The furrows in her forehead showed me the deep concern she felt over what she was sharing. "I've been shut off all my life—always living alone. I want things to be different now!"

Ethel Waters had lived her life in the lonely existence that only those in the public limelight know. In addition to this, never having a family with which to share her joys and sorrows forced her to turn inward most of her life. Even her closest friends never knew the real person behind the celebrity.

Another hazard of her profession was the constant lack of privacy. When everyone recognizes you, it becomes a struggle to shop, to go to church, to go out to a restaurant, or to accomplish any of the simple tasks we take for granted. Some famous people revel in the attention, but Mom Waters did not.

She barely tolerated signing autographs, sometimes refusing to give them. She shunned parties and, aside from a few very close friends in the entertainment field, preferred to spend her time in the company of unknowns. She dreaded interviews, for fear of being misquoted and hurting someone or having her thoughts about her Saviour misinterpreted.

All these factors were made more difficult by severe health problems, and therefore she retreated to the haven of her apartment, where she lived alone and undisturbed. She learned that Jesus Christ was all she needed.

Actually, it wasn't difficult to get along with her, as long as one had respect for her Lord and was aware of the few things she absolutely would not tolerate. I jokingly called them her pet peeves.

The first might seem trivial, but to her it was tremendously important. She simply could not stand to be called *Mrs.* Waters! I recall the uncomfortable feeling I got as I watched people with good intentions address her as "Mrs. Waters." The retort was always the same—she would *never* let it go by.

"It's Miss. M-I-S-S!" she would reply. Then, as if to make up, she would nonchalantly add with a chuckle, "Don't ruin my chances!"

Ethel Waters never knew her father, but she went by his name, even though her parents were never married. She had married and loved several men at various times during her career, but all the relationships terminated with a broken heart and bitter disappointments.

When she loved, she loved deeply. When she was hurt, the bitterness ate away like acid, until the Lord Jesus Christ came into her life and took it away. He became the Partner and Companion she had longed for and sought after for so many lonely years.

The other thing that she definitely would not tolerate was the use of the word *black* in referring to her people. She refused to polarize humans into black and white. I never gave any thought to the difference in our races, and so our children grew in their relationship with her, not realizing any difference either. I remember the time one of our daughters revealed her attitude to me. She was a preschooler at the time and had some questions about the differences in people's skin coloring. In Sunday school they had been singing about the fact that God makes people of all colors.

"Yes, honey, that's right," I said. "Like Grandma Waters. Her skin is brown."

"Oh, Mommie," she laughed, running off to play, "Grandma Waters doesn't have brown skin. Her skin is just like ours!"

Mom believed with all her heart that God is color-blind and not class-conscious. "I'll admit that when I was young I didn't like white people," she said one day. Since then, the Lord had removed her deep-seated bitterness and replaced it with love.

On another occasion she reinforced these feelings: "I never separate blacks and whites—it's people and sin that count. When you get right with God, you forget all that foolishness!"

Unfortunately some of Mom's race misunderstood her strong feelings, and she was accused more than once of being against the black cause. Nothing could be further from the truth. She was fiercely proud of her race. "I'm proud to be a Negress!" she told a reporter during one interview. "I'm not concerned with civil rights," she said. "I'm only concerned with God-given rights, and they are available to everyone!"

Her feelings could be summed up by what she told me

one day while we were discussing a television program on racial prejudice. She turned and said, "Baby, I want to be known first of all as Ethel Waters, a Christian, and then as an American, and then as a member of the Negro race—in that order! People get their priorities all mixed up!"

As I sat beside her, listening to her every breath, I marveled at the unique individual she was. Through her example and strength of personality, she reinforced what I had been taught as a child. I too am uniquely made, according to God's design—special in my appearance, talent, and personality. It was my responsibility to make the most of what He had already given me, and to make my life count for His honor and glory.

5

Just a Closer Walk

I am weak, but Thou art strong!
Jesus, keep me from all wrong,
I'll be satisfied as long
As I walk, let me walk,
Close to Thee!

TRADITIONAL SPIRITUAL

The regular, soft groanings that came with each gasp of breath suddenly became much louder, accompanied by an increase in restlessness.

I reluctantly glanced at the clock, which had become my enemy during this night as I sat and watched the minutes ruthlessly rushing by. It was 4:00 A.M., and this, together with the change in the condition of my patient, told me the injection I had administered earlier was wearing off and another was needed. I moved to prepare the medication I felt assured would bring the relief so desperately needed. I leaned close to her haggard face and whispered her name to arouse her, not wanting to startle her by administering the injection without a warning.

"I'm going to give you a shot now, Mom. It's what the doctor ordered to help you," I said reassuringly. The needle went through the soft skin with ease, and she groaned pathetically as the fluid stung the delicate tissues below the skin.

As I administered the medication, a slight twinge of guilt passed through my mind. I recalled how she dreaded the thought of taking medicine of any kind. In all my years as a nurse, I had never seen a patient who disliked taking pills as much as Ethel Waters. She even rebelled against taking vitamins! This seemed to come from her years of living in the midst of poverty and vice and seeing strong, vibrant people change into useless individuals under the influence of drugs.

Even when the suffering was intense, she would pointedly watch the clock and not take the much-needed medication a second before the allotted time. She wanted no part of having her body and mind controlled by medication. Instead of taking additional relief when the pain became intense, she would say, "I'll just lie here and talk to my precious Jesus, and ask Him to please ease the pain a little!"

The shock of the sharp needle temporarily brought her out of her stuporous condition. "Precious Jesus— Merciful Father!" she called quietly over and over again, writhing in pain. "Oh, my Father, help me! Oh, precious Jesus, be merciful to me!"

Searching for some way to help, I prepared a wet

washcloth and began wiping her face, arms, and hands, talking to her softly all the time, reassuring her of my love.

"Precious Jesus—Merciful Father!" The moaning continued between gasps for air.

Completely frustrated and exhausted, I cried out from the depths of my soul, "God, have mercy on Your dear child! Take her home, please," I pleaded. "Quickly, Lord! What is the sense in this? Why let her linger? Please, Father!"

My eyes suddenly fell on the open Bible lying on the dresser across the room. "Why didn't you think of it sooner?" I reproached myself, remembering the many times I had read to her in the past to soothe and comfort her through long days. I had used the Bible the afternoon before, when the suffering was intense, and watched as the pain subsided and relaxation came. I didn't have to ask which portion to read. It was always the same—Psalm 71. I sat down next to the bed with the open Bible in my lap.

"Mom, I'm going to read to you." I knew she heard me, because a slight smile came over her face and her breathing became easier as she strained to hear the first beloved word. I carefully thumbed through the worn Bible until I found the chapter I had memorized from daily reading. As I looked closely at it through the dim light, the meaning of the words struck me as never before, and I wondered whether this would be the last time I would read this portion of Scripture to my wonderful friend.

I noticed that the heading under the chapter number was "A Prayer for Old Age." No wonder it had been such a comfort for one living in the solitude of an apartment, unable to get out—a solitude only the elderly can understand.

I recalled the day I questioned Mom about the special significance of this one portion. "Why does it mean so much to you?" I asked. "It is a beautiful portion of God's Word, but there are others equally as beautiful."

"Well, honey, it goes way back," she began, throwing her head back and gazing off in the distance with a look that told me the memory was painful. "It was one of the lowest points of my life. I was lonely, desperate, and bitter from wrongs committed against me—a long string of them, too painful to mention. One night I sat alone in my hotel room, feeling terribly sorry for myself. I was discouraged and fearful, and my heart was breaking, while off in the distance I heard people laughing and having fun at a party.

"In desperation I turned to a Bible sitting on the table—this was before I committed my life to Jesus. I cried out to God to help me, and I opened the Bible at random to the Psalms. My eyes fell on Psalm Seventy-one. It was a turning point in my life! The words fit my situation exactly and they spoke to my heart and comforted me in such a wonderful way that I felt they were written especially for me. Ever since then, it has been *my* Psalm!"

I began reading slowly to Mom, wanting it to bring much-needed comfort and to provide the therapy that drugs had failed to supply. Attempting to make it last as long as possible, I paused frequently after certain verses to reflect on their meaning in the life of my patient.

In thee, O Lord, do I put my trust: let me never be put to confusion.

Psalms 71:1

The Lord had certainly granted her that prayer. As I looked at her that night I saw a decrepit body, worn with age and illness. But encased in that body was a young, alert, and vibrant mind—not at all put to confusion!

Be thou my strong habitation, whereunto I may continually resort: thou hast given commandment to save me; for thou art my rock and my fortress.

Verse 3

Ethel Waters learned at a very early age that there was no human on earth she could depend on, and gradually she learned to depend on the God of Creation. Because of the circumstances surrounding her birth, her mother resented her. She turned for security to her maternal grandmother, who loved her. But the grandmother worked as a live-in domestic and was home only one day a week. Soon she died of cancer, leaving no one to love her granddaughter.

There were two neighborhood churches that little Ethel attended, receiving the friendship and acceptance her young heart craved. One was the Roman Catholic church, where the sisters were kind and loving to her. The other was the Baptist church on the corner, a place she liked to be, as the people seemed to have a spirit she was attracted to.

At the age of twelve, she responded to an altar call and

received Jesus Christ as her personal Saviour. However, the experience was dampened when she was wrongfully treated by another teenager in the church. She never went back.

The bitterness of that experience lasted for years. It was always with her as she traveled the road leading to success, but so was the knowledge that she belonged to the Lord and should be serving Him.

For thou art my hope, O Lord God: thou art my trust from my youth. By thee have I been holden up from the womb: thou art he that took me out of my mother's bowels: my praise shall be continually of thee.

Verses 5, 6

It has been said that no other performer ever came out of a childhood that was so dark and so cold. Ethel Waters' career, indeed her whole life, had been a series of highs and lows—until she met her Saviour.

It was a lonely road, which led all the way from the worst slums of Chester, Pennsylvania, to the floodlights of Carnegie Hall; from earning four dollars a week as a scullion to being the highest-paid Negro performer on Broadway; from singing in the back room of saloons to being invited to entertain at the White House; from roaming unnoticed in the dirty streets of the slums to appearing before millions on radio, TV, stage, and screen.

But along with the fame, material wealth, and professional respect came bitterness, loneliness, resentment, racial prejudice, and disappointment in a long list of people.

> I am as a wonder unto many; but thou art my strong
> refuge.
>
>   Verse 7

I paused in my reading to glance up from the printed page. How helpless she looked, but even now she was a true wonder to people all over the world.

She came into prominence at a time when it was almost impossible for a Negro artist to achieve critical recognition in a white-dominated field, developing into a noted singer, comic, dancer, and dramatic actress. She was a complete all-around performer. Acclaimed by critics as an entertainer unlimited, she felt as comfortable singing in front of a few friends as singing in front of world leaders.

Ethel Waters began earning money for the essentials of living as a child by running errands for the prostitutes who lived and worked in the ghetto where she grew up. She had little adult supervision. "We were a rough bunch of kids," she said once. "But we weren't perverse or immoral. The adults around us lived in their own vices, but they didn't mistreat us kids. They simply allowed us to live our own lives."

She continued, "And we had respect for God and our country. But when I think now of the trouble we could have gotten into, I know God had His hand on me even then!"

In her early teens she entered into an unhappy marriage to please her family. The marriage lasted only a few years, and during that time she worked as a chambermaid. It was while doing the tedious tasks of her job that she began imitating well-known entertainers in front of the large mirrors she was required to clean.

One night she was invited to a party and coaxed into entertaining everyone with one of the routines she had created. There she was discovered by two small-time agents, and bookings began to come in—slowly at first, and then gradually increasing in number and importance. At times it was very discouraging, but she had the talent and the determination to make it the hard way.

Ethel Waters' life really contained three careers. The first began as a singer over sixty years ago, when she first sang "St. Louis Blues" at the Lincoln Theater in Baltimore. She spent several years traveling in the South, appearing with numerous vaudeville acts and doing song-and-dance routines as "Sweet Mama Stringbean."

In her younger years, her voice truly depicted the sparrow for which she later became famous. Her vocal range was very broad—from a smoldering, throaty growl to caressingly clear, tender upper tones that enveloped and embraced a melody. She was a master at controlling her voice, making it do anything she wanted it to do. She made famous such songs as "Stormy Weather," "Heat Wave," "Dinah," "Am I Blue?" "Cabin in the Sky," "Supper Time," and the ever-famous "His Eye Is on the Sparrow."

Her first musical on Broadway was *Africana*. She then appeared in several Broadway revues and musicals, including *Blackbirds, Rhapsody in Black, As Thousands*

Cheer, and *At Home Abroad.*

It was not until the 1930s that she emerged as a dramatic actress, which was her second career. In the year
1939 she appeared in *Mamba's Daughters.* This was followed by *Cabin in the Sky, Pinky,* and her most famous
Broadway performance and movie role as Bernice in
Member of the Wedding. She was acclaimed as one of
the greatest performers the American theater has ever
produced, and still heads the list of stars studied by
high-school students across the country.

> Cast me not off in the time of old age; forsake me not
> when my strength faileth. For mine enemies speak
> against me; and they that lay wait for my soul take
> counsel together, Saying, God hath forsaken him:
> persecute and take him; for there is none to deliver
> him. O God, be not far from me: O my God, make
> haste for my help.
>
> Verses 9–12

It was during the 1950s, after her successful performance in *Member of the Wedding,* that Ethel Waters hit
her all-time low. After the curtain calls were over, she
left the theater to face an empty hotel room and to spend
the long nights alone. She knew better than anyone that
loneliness is one of mankind's greatest miseries!

6

Each Step of the Way

There were times I had trials and tribulations;
I was lost in a world of trouble and sin,
But I found so many revelations,
When the beautiful heavenly light shone in.
He's guiding my feet to walk uprightly,
He's opening my heart to sing and to pray,
I know that Jesus is holding my hand—how can I falter?
When—He's with me . . . each step of the Way.

REGINALD BEANE

In the 1950s, Ethel Waters' career began lagging and her personal life was a disappointment, so the Sweet Mama Stringbean of the past turned to food for the comfort she needed—and soon found herself weighing over 375 pounds! Unable to adjust emotionally to such a huge body and finding it difficult to work while carrying around so much weight, she continued to turn inward, with more bitterness and discouragement.

While working in New York City in 1957, she attended the Billy Graham Crusade one night. She was so touched that she came back to every single meeting for sixteen weeks. During that time, all of the questions that haunted her were answered, and, regretting the wasted years of living without Him, she recommitted her heart and life to her Saviour and purposed in her heart to channel all of her energies into serving Him. From then on, things would be different!

But I will hope continually, and will yet praise thee more and more.

Verse 14

Jesus Christ quickly became the center of her life, and absolutely everything revolved around her relationship with Him. The press reported that Ethel Waters had become deeply religious, but she disagreed.

"I'm not religious. I'm a born-again Christian!" she proudly declared. "That's the most important thing in my life, because I've found my living Saviour!"

Facing the same question everyone has to face, that of "What will you do with Jesus Christ?" her decision was: "I trust Him by faith as my Saviour. The same faith that I show in a chair when I sit down, that it can hold all three hundred and eighty pounds of me! My Saviour is a good company keeper. I am completely His."

One day she stated, "I was converted when I was twelve, but then I got away from it. I know the side of life without Him. I had fame, but I was empty." She found that Jesus Christ can change a bitter, miserable person into something beautiful, as she gave Him the heavy load of problems she had carried all of her life. The freedom she felt as they rolled off was invigorating.

"It was important to me to find out, before it was too late, what my purpose in living was, and what my Lord and Saviour Jesus Christ wanted from me. We go through life not knowing, not believing, not claiming the promises of God. I know by faith, and I believe that there is a Saviour. I am at peace!" From then on, Mom lavished on Him all the love she had saved up inside herself from a lifetime of loneliness.

O God, thou hast taught me from my youth: and hitherto have I declared thy wondrous works. Now also when I am old and greyheaded, O God, forsake me not; until I have shewed thy strength unto this generation, and thy power to every one that is to come.

                                                Verses 17, 18

Ethel Waters never acted a role or rendered a song unless in some way she had experienced it in her own life—it had to be *her*. When she sang or acted about heartbreak, it was because she had known heartbreak all her life.

"People acclaim my acting ability," she once laughingly remarked. "I'm not such a good actress—I've just got a good memory!"

After her 1957 dedication to serving the Lord, she declared, "I can't sing the blues and 'Stormy Weather' anymore, because my life isn't stormy now. The Saviour has put sunshine in my life! I don't want to sing the songs that remind me of when I had heartbreaks." So, aside from a few scattered roles playing parts she felt could bring honor to her Saviour, the great Ethel Waters left the theater and devoted the rest of her life to serving Christ. This was the beginning of her third career.

"There's so much in the world today, and in the theater, that is Sodom and Gomorrah. It's the devil's kingdom, and he's doing a pretty good job of reigning!" The joy of her newfound life-style was perfectly summed up when she jokingly said, "I'm not a part of the Jet Set any longer, but I *am* a member of the God Set!"

With her newfound joy and commitment came a fierce intolerance for any disrespect for the Lord. She did not expect a person to believe the way she did, but she would demand respect for what she believed. She explained it this way: "I love to talk about my Jesus, but I won't cram Him down anybody's throat. He's much too precious for that. I don't mind if people think I'm a kook, because I won't sell my Saviour cheap. That's Ethel Waters," she'd proudly defend when explaining to someone her feelings about the Lord. "What you believe is your business. I happen to love Him and believe in Him. I don't care to argue about it. You can feel the way you want to and respect me for the way I feel!"

She summed up her feelings about leaving the theater when she said, "People ask if I miss the theater. The answer is *no!* The professional world of my day was good to me. The fans loved me, and I loved them. But you are a servant of the public, and you can't please everybody all the time. You can always please Jesus!"

Thou, which hast shewed me great and sore troubles, shalt quicken me again, and shalt bring me up again from the depths of the earth.

Verse 20

"Julie! Stop. Read that again," she had sobbed the day before while I was reading this same portion of Scripture to her. "Do you really believe that?" she had asked, her eyes filled with longing to see an end to her suffering.

"Of course I believe it, Mom. And so do you. God loves you," I reassured her. "You know that better than anyone. And when it's time for Him to lift you up, He'll surely do it."

The look of comfort which flooded her eyes was similar to the look which faintly took shape that night. She didn't open her eyes or respond in any way verbally, but I knew from her calmness that she was hearing every word I read.

My mouth shall shew forth thy righteousness and thy salvation all the day . . . .
Verse 15

I paused to contemplate what I had just read, looking at those lips, now so still, that had in the last several years never ceased to offer praise to her precious Saviour. This was another lesson, perhaps the best and most practical of all, that she had taught me—that my Saviour is with me, moment by moment, interested in every detail of my day. He's down here with me, where life is—willing to be with me and go with me through everything!

Ethel Waters was ever mindful that her Saviour was by her side. She held constant conversation and communion with Him, giving Him credit for every blessing and trusting Him with every little problem that came her way. She uttered His name in almost every breath. "I give the Lord all the credit for everything I've done, or ever will do. I have such gratitude! It's nothing I do, baby," she said with a smile. "It's God!"

We became accustomed to Mom's constant conversations with the Lord. Sometimes right in the middle of a sentence, she would turn her face heavenward and hold private, or sometimes open, chats with her Lord. She would explain: "The Lord and I have a running conversation. He makes no errors. I do, but He takes me anyway!"

It didn't matter how small a decision was, she always sought an answer from the Lord. For big decisions she always said, "I'll give an answer later," and then she consulted with God and waited for His answer. Once, commenting on this, she said, "If Ethel will just stop talking and get quiet before the Lord, that 'still, small voice' will come through to me. And Jesus knows that, to the best of my abilities, that's the one I listen to!"

Many times when the suffering was intense and the doctor would ask the proverbial, "Well, Miss Waters, how are you doing?" she would chuckle and answer, "Oh, Doctor, thanks to my blessed Saviour, I've got no complaints."

With her deep commitment and love for her Lord came the burning desire to study the Word of God and learn from it. Although it was impossible to attend church because of her physical condition and the stir her presence caused among the congregation, she loved to listen to her favorite people teaching the Word of God on the radio. Not leaning toward any denomination, she

called these radio teachers her pastors, and often com-
municated with them.

Her Bibles, so worn and ragged-looking on the shelf,
showed the hours and hours they were studied. Oswald
Chambers' *My Utmost for His Highest* was the book she
loved best, next to the Bible.

Along with her love for the Saviour came a mindful-
ness of His adversary. Ethel Waters accepted the fact
that there is a strong evil force operating in the world.
She openly warned people about it.

"The devil has never forgiven me for letting him
down—we were buddy-buddy for so long," she laughingly admitted. "He's constantly trying to trip me up. He
comes in so many different ways. He's got guile! If I take
my eyes off the Lord, I can feel myself slipping!"

Thou shalt increase my greatness, and comfort me
on every side . . . . unto thee will I sing . . . O
thou Holy One of Israel. My lips shall greatly rejoice
when I sing unto thee; and my soul, which thou hast
redeemed.

Verses 21–23

After her commitment to Jesus Christ, Ethel Waters
was still a tremendously magnetic performer, and she
threw herself into her newfound career of serving Him
with all the remaining strength she had. "When you get
to know Him, you can't keep from raving about Him.
Any time I get a chance to open my mouth and make a
loud voice for my Saviour, that's my thing," she once
told the president of the United States.

She began traveling from coast to coast in a new kind
of ministry—putting on Christian concerts. Only this
time as she enthralled audiences, this time as she
traveled, this time as she faced the empty hotel room at
night, she was not alone. She had a Partner.

Her audience would assemble, watching in silence as
the big lady struggled to walk toward the podium at
center stage. Upon arriving, she would look straight at
her audience and break out in that great contagious grin,
saying simply, "Hi!"

If the answer coming back wasn't exuberant enough,
she would repeat it as many times as necessary to get the
response that told her the audience was totally with her.
Soon the music would join in, and she would begin to
sing in soft, meaningful tones about her Lord.

> Oh, it's wonderful, to have God as your
>   partner,
> And He'll always be by your side.
> And when the road is rough,
> And things get tough,
> He'll come along just for the ride!

The audience would sit mesmerized as she put forth
her tremendous power of communication and sang from
the depths of a soul once deeply scarred, but now
healed.

> If you have faith in Him, He will guide
>   and protect you,
> Share your joy or pain.

And when the future is dim;
Invest in Him;
And He'll bring you out of the rain!

Those piercing eyes would focus on individuals in the audience, making each person feel as if he were being personally seen to. She would point and shake a finger directly at certain people.

If you'll just put your trust in the Lord
    forever,
And discard worry and fear,
If you'll believe in Him,
You will forever
Be able to smile through your tears!

The message came across clear and strong as she projected the truth behind those sermons in song. "Mom knows what she's talking about, dear children, so listen carefully," she warned.

It's wonderful to have God for a partner!
And in Him alone, at any time, you can confide.
As it's never too late, for Him to give you
    that break,
When you're partners with God.

Bursts of laughter would alternate with quiet as the listeners soaked up the message. It was coming from a person who had gained victory over a broken heart; it was going to those whose hearts were still bleeding.

Tho' avoided, shunned, sometimes branded
  a failure,
Not one open door to be found.
If you'll only believe! Just believe!
That miracles can happen, He will regain
  your lost crown.
I tell you, you just can't lose, with God
  as your partner,
And in simple humble faith in Him (through
  His Son Jesus)
Is your only plea.

Many in the audience would have tears streaming
down their cheeks as Ethel Waters was used by the
Spirit to convict and convince—through a personalized
message.

So darlings, why must you delay?
Begin this (right now!) this very day!
Being partners with God!
  ETHEL WATERS AND EDDIE STUART

As the music softly concluded, she would speak ten-
derly, directly into the microphone. "He loves you. And
so do I!"

One scene from a long and varied career which included stage plays, television, and nightclub acts. Here Ethel, Lillian Gish, and Janice Rule played in the TV production of *The Sound and the Fury. (Photograph by United Press International.)*

Fame alone was empty for Ethel. As she rededicated her life to God, she found that He could make a bitter, miserable life into something beautiful.

Ethel proved herself to be a legend in her own age; she was an actress, singer, humorist, and entertainer par excellence.

Singing was one of the joys of Ethel Waters' life. Reginald Beane was both a dear friend and accompanist.

A complex personality was one of the trademarks of this performer. Through her strong faith in Him, God was able to richly use and bless this multifaceted woman. (*Photograph by Martha Holmes.*)

A smiling Ethel poses beside her beloved piano in her home in Pasadena.

"Mom" Waters seemed to have enough love for many children. Julie Harris received a warm hug and the gift of an open heart. *Below:* Ethel was always particular about the way she looked, but serving the Lord was more important to her than any earthly possessions.

Ethel Waters and the author in 1964 outside Ethel's home in
Pasadena.

Famous people, even presidents, were Ethel's friends. Evangelist Billy Graham escorted her to the White House wedding of Tricia Nixon. (*Photograph by United Press International.*)

After her recommitment to Jesus Christ, Ethel Waters was still a tremendously magnetic performer. She always encouraged her audience to "choose now." *Below:* Giving was an important part of Ethel Waters' life. "Where I'm going, I won't need anything," she declared. Here Juliann DeKorte plays Ethel's piano, which "Mom" gave to the DeKortes before she died.

7

Homesick for Heaven

I'm a pilgrim; I'm a stranger;
Just traveling through
This barren land.
I've got a home in yonder city,
That's not made by mortal man.
TRADITIONAL SPIRITUAL

As the last hollow tones of my weary voice trailed off
into the darkness of early morning, my patient gave forth
a long sigh of satisfaction. The injection, combined with
the soothing words from her favorite portion of Scripture, brought a momentary lull in the storm of suffering.

She nodded her head, indicating agreement with the
message just completed. As I watched closely, I could
see that she was attempting to speak, and I leaned close
to her pale face, trying to decipher the faint whisper.

At first I couldn't make out what the parched lips were
forming, then gradually I realized it was the same thing
she had said to me many times before, with a look of
longing and anticipation in her eyes. Slowly, over and

over again, she murmured, "I . . . want . . . to go . . . *home!*"

Trying to swallow back my tears, I reached out and stroked the familiar forehead. "I know, Mom. I know. Jesus knows that, too. He'll let you go when it's His time. Let's just leave it up to Him. Okay?"

She nodded her head and seemed to relax, giving in to her body's natural urge to live, even though her spirit was anxious to take leave.

I leafed through the torn and worn pages of her beloved Bible, noticing passages where she had obviously spent a great deal of time in study and meditation. They were set apart by markings and notes written in the margin. I could easily tell how precious this Bible was to her.

I continued to explore the book, searching out passages for my own encouragement as I sat and waited at the bedside. Soon my eyes fell on the inscription in the front, written by the person who gave the Bible to her many years before. It read: *"This book belongs to: Ethel Waters. Address: Everywhere."*

"How true!" I marveled. I knew that whoever wrote this understood the same Mom Waters I did.

Ethel Waters never had a home, although she always longed for a place where she could feel safe, a place where she belonged. She desired a home where she could live with her family and where all could meet at the end of the day and find love and acceptance, receive encouragement, and fellowship with one another. As a child she was never given a home; as an adult she desperately sought after the home she desired; but none was to be found.

Ethel Waters was born on Halloween, October 31, 1896, to a girl of twelve who had been raped by a friend of her sister. All during little Ethel's childhood, her mother, only a child herself, bounced her to and fro around the city, sending her to live first with one relative and then with another. But Ethel, who was always large for her age, never seemed to fit in anywhere. No one really wanted her.

She grew out of childhood carrying a deep-seated desire to have a home of her own. But the years passed, and the rugged transient life of an entertainer robbed her of fulfillment of this desire. She was once again thrust to and fro, only this time across the country, living most of the time in rooming houses and cheap hotels. She could perform at the nice hotels, but not eat or sleep in them because of her race.

Two unsuccessful marriages failed to produce the home that she was trying to establish. Later, as an adult, she joyfully purchased the house of her dreams in Los Angeles, only to be working in New York City most of the time she owned it. Eventually it was snatched away by that nightmare of our modern cities—the heartless freeway.

By the time she reached her fifties, having a home of her own seemed hopeless, and living in lonely despair seemed the only solution. Then Jesus Christ took control, and everything was changed.

"What made me come to Jesus was, I was just plain homesick!" she once commented.

When God Almighty became her Heavenly Father, and His Son, Jesus Christ, her partner, she joined the large family of people who have a common home—a heavenly home. Heaven was her Father's abode, and by inheritance her rightful home. The truth of this found its place in her heart. From then on, her desire for an earthly home was no longer important, and to be with her Lord in her heavenly home became her hope and goal.

Ever since Ethel Waters had committed her life to the Lord, she had lived in constant anticipation of the moment she would meet her Saviour face-to-face and live forever in the home prepared for her. She never complained about the length of time it was taking, but rather used each day to work for her Lord and spread His Good News until His perfect time to take her came. The longing was always there, however, and she talked frequently of going home.

"I'm just plain homesick for heaven, sweetheart!" she said to me one day. "I'm ready to go when my Lord calls me!"

When we brought her to our house, we all quickly adjusted to a workable routine. She seemed to revel in the noise and activity of a busy family just before Christmas—the very thing I was so afraid would bother her. She excitedly gave me the money to buy each person who would be at our home on Christmas Day a present. "I want something that will last—something they'll look at and remember me."

Although she was unable to sit and could only walk a

few steps to the bathroom and back to bed, she was in constant contact with everything that took place in the house. It wasn't interference, but rather a keen interest in being a part of the family, not just a bystander looking on.

She loved the smells of Christmas baking, the Christmas music that filled the house, and the dog barking in excitement every time the front doorbell rang.

"Julie," she called loudly one day as I was working in the kitchen.

I wiped my hands and walked quickly to her room. "Yes, Mom?"

"I can, smell you're baking something. Let's see—it smells like pumpkin pie!" she said with a sly look.

"Would you like some, Mom?" I asked.

"No, not now. Maybe later. But save me some. I just wanted you to know you weren't puttin' something over on me!" Then she threw back her head and laughed heartily.

Christmas morning dawned crisp and cool. The children sneaked down the stairs with whispered excitement just as the sun peeked through, and then they waited impatiently while the adults crawled out of bed and stumbled down in robes and slippers. There were eight of us enjoying the jubilation that morning.

Mom Waters wasn't able to join us around the tree, but with the double doors to her room flung open, she could look across the entryway into the living room and see everything. She sat propped up in her bed, beaming as she enjoyed the festivities.

I wondered if she had ever been to such a joyous

Christmas celebration. The children showed her each present they opened, and she would enthusiastically approve. Soon it was time for her to open her gift, and we all stood around the bed watching as she squealed with delight.

The turkey and sweet potatoes baking in the oven began filling the house with a delicious aroma. The logs crackled as they burned in the fireplace, and beautiful carols came from the stereo.

Before eating our Christmas breakfast, we joined together in prayer, giving thanks for our family and the privilege of being together for the birthday celebration of our Saviour. We also remembered our special family member in bed in the other room, asking that soon she would be strengthened enough to join us around the table. We eagerly began to dig into the scrambled eggs, sausage, and coffee cake. Paul, looking toward the kitchen door, suddenly said, "Well, look who's here!"

Everyone's head turned in the direction of the doorway. There was Mom Waters, leaning heavily on the sash, beaming proudly at her accomplishment of making it all the way to the back of the house by herself to surprise us!

She could tell how delighted we all were—this was the best Christmas present of all! She lifted one hand toward heaven and slowly, with much difficulty, began to sing, "Jesus, we just want to thank You!"

We all joined in, trying to choke back the tears, giving honor to the One to whom it belonged on that Christmas Day. We wouldn't have taken any vocal awards on that morning, but we sang, "Thank You for being so good!"

I walked over to help Mom back into her room. She was completely exhausted after the effort of walking such a distance alone for the first time in months. That was the first and last time Mom would walk into any room of our home. She would never gain enough strength to join us at the dinner table; she would never walk unassisted again. And instead of gaining the strength we prayed for on Christmas Day, she would gradually become weaker and weaker.

As I tucked her back into bed that morning, she laid her head wearily on the pillow and said, "Thank You, Jesus. You helped me do it!"

Later that night, after everyone was in bed, the noisy house quiet, and the ribbons and wrappings put away, she said, "Thank you, Julie. This was the nicest Christmas I've ever had."

"Oh, Mom," I exclaimed, "don't thank me. *You're* the one who made our Christmas special. You completed the circle. We want to thank you."

The days stretched into weeks, and Mom made no improvement. Her spirits were good, but the pain was relentless, and further complications set in. It soon became obvious that she could never live alone again and that we should make plans for a permanent arrangement.

We gingerly approached the subject of giving up her apartment, as it seemed ridiculous for her to spend money keeping it. As usual, she wanted to think about it for a while. The Lord would have to do the work in her heart. We realized how very difficult it is for older people to give up their own place—their last source of independence.

A few days later she said, "I've been thinking about what you children said about giving up my apartment. The Lord has told me that it is the right thing to do. I'd like to move here as many of my things as possible. You know I love my clothes and furniture, and I'd like to have them close, even though I can't use them. Just to look at them will be a joy."

So we began the difficult task of dismantling a fifteenth-floor apartment without the owner being present. With a telephone at her bedside and one in the apartment, we could receive instructions as frequently as needed. This gave her the opportunity to direct the whole project.

The small things were moved gradually, but finally the big day arrived when the furniture was moved. With the excitement of a war bride being reunited with her husband, she greeted each beloved piece of furniture. Eyes sparkling, she called out instructions as to where each piece was to be placed. Everything possible was crammed into her one room, but the beautiful baby grand piano, sofa, and huge philodendron plant were put in the living room, where she could easily see and enjoy them from her bed. At last all was in order.

"Now I can rest," she exclaimed. "Everything is here!"

Somehow it was mistakenly reported that she had to give up her apartment because of financial reasons. Nothing could be further from the truth! Ethel Waters always insisted on paying her own way. When I asked her to please stay with us as our guest, she wrinkled up her face and scolded me. "Julie, I thought you knew me.

But I guess you don't, or you would know that I *must* pay my own way. All my life I've paid my own way, and that of my family. Don't take that away from me now, or I'll have to struggle up out of this bed and leave here!"

I could tell she was serious. This was very important to her, so we agreed on an amount, and she did indeed pay her own way.

Aside from her physical discomforts, which made living unbearable anywhere, Mom was happy with us. But it still wasn't her home. That was yet to come.

That last night, as I looked down at her, I could see the homesickness written on her face as she waited patiently to be released from her tired body. I was reminded of the verse in the Bible:

> For we have not an high priest which cannot be touched with the feeling of our infirmities; but was in all points tempted like as we are, yet without sin.
>
> Hebrews 4:15

Yes, Jesus understood what it was to be homesick. He left the glories of His heavenly home, which was filled with happiness and wonder unspeakable, and came to this sin-sick earth to suffer and die for the sins of the world. He had no home here, either. How He must have longed to be back with His Father in heaven!

> Sometimes I feel like a motherless child,
> A long, long way from home.

8

Nobody Knows
but Jesus

Sometimes I feel discouraged,
Sometimes the shadows fall,
Sometimes my heart feels lonely,
And longs for heaven and home.
With Jesus as my partner,
My constant friend is He,
For His eye is on the sparrow,
And I know He watches me!

MRS. C. B. MARTIN

The clock pointed to 5:15, and I realized why once again I felt smothered by weariness. From working many night shifts, I knew that the hour just before dawn is the most difficult time to stay awake.

I got up to stretch and walked around to the other side of the bed. As I did, the volume of the radio suddenly increased, something that frequently happens at night, and I could hear a man singing "What a Friend We Have in Jesus." The words soothed my troubled mind and filled me with new hope and comfort.

I paced back and forth across the room, trying to shake off the drowsiness. My patient's condition appeared to be worsening, and thoughts came crowding in to confuse me. As I continued to walk slowly, the strains of the soft music filled my ears. The familiar words flowed out of the radio and directly into my heart, as if they were meant especially for me.

> Are you weak and heavy laden?
> 'Cumbered with a load of care?
> Jesus knows our every weakness.
> Take it to the Lord in prayer.
>
> JOSEPH SCRIVEN

My knees gave way and I dropped to the floor, pouring out all the frustrations and fears in my heart that morning. True to His Word, He became my strength and my hope. His peace flooded my soul.

I wasn't aware of how long I knelt by the bed, but soon I realized that the groaning had resumed and was steadily rising in intensity. The medication was no longer controlling the discomfort. If I gave her another injection now, her blood pressure and breathing might be affected. I took her hand, saying, "I'm still here, Mom. I know it hurts. The Lord knows, too, and He'll help you."

Very slowly she moved her head toward me and opened her mouth, trying to speak. The words slurred together, barely discernible, but I will never forget them. With opened eyes focusing on nothing, she said what were to be her last words to me.

"Julie. I . . . love . . . you!"

I cautiously sat on the edge of the bed, trying not to cause further discomfort. The tears ran down my cheeks as I leaned forward and softly kissed her moist forehead. "Mom, I love you, too."

Frustrated, I looked around for something that needed to be done, something tangible I could do to help—but there was nothing. I remembered someone telling me long ago, "When you can't do nursing, you can do a lot of loving."

No longer feeling useless, I sat down and held her hand, talking softly to ears I was sure could still hear. I reassured her of my presence, my love, and most of all, the love of her Lord and Saviour.

Suffering was nothing new to Ethel Waters. She had endured it all her life. It came to her in two forms— emotional and physical—and it seemed she had more than her share of each.

I never knew Ethel Waters when she was in good health. Her severe physical problems began twenty years before, triggered by her obesity. Along with making it impossible to walk normally, the extra weight brought the severe complications of diabetes, congestive heart failure, hypertension, anemia, dizziness, and arterial sclerotic heart disease. These all eventually led to cataracts and partial blindness, thrombophlebitis and diabetic neuritis.

Most of her last twenty years were spent in bed, except when traveling to give concerts or taking an occasional trip to a store or the doctor.

It was difficult for her to get around during those first few years after committing her life to Christ. This frustrated her a great deal, because she wanted to be telling of her newfound joy.

The first thing she set out to accomplish after recommitting her life to God was to lose the extra weight. It was sometimes discouraging, but gradually she dropped from a high of 380 pounds to 160! It was a slow descent over several years, but added up at last to a loss of 220 pounds.

Many people made a big fuss over the weight loss and sought her out for her "secret." To Mom the secret was simple. When she gave her life to Jesus, all the things that were unrestrained came under control.

"I ate correctly, stayed under my doctor's care, and most of all, prayed to my Heavenly Father for strength to say *no!*"

Just when it became easier for her to move around with a slimmer body, she began to grow weaker from the effects of diabetes. Her vision was helped by two separate cataract surgeries, and thick glasses were prescribed, but gradually her eyes continued to worsen, until once again she could see very little.

Because of her heart condition, surgery on her cancer could not be performed, and the alternative was eight weeks of intense radiation therapy and permanent chemotherapy. This arrested the spread of the cancer, but caused permanent damage in the surrounding tissues. She was to later endure the complications of blood clots and kidney failure.

Always a proud woman, meticulous in her personal

grooming and attire, it was humiliating to her to become physically incapacitated. To be so helpless with such a strong personality—to be dependent on others when she had always been independent—was degrading. To have her body grow old when her mind refused to age was frustrating. To deteriorate when she yearned to be active was depressing.

"I can take the blindness," she once commented. "I can take not being able to sit, and I can take the pain. But what is so difficult is having to lie here and not be able to sing for my Lord anymore!"

However, true to His Word, God had provided her with ways of escape.

No temptation has overtaken you but such as is common to man; and God is faithful, who will not allow you to be tempted beyond what you are able, but with the temptation will provide the way of escape also, that you may be able to endure it.

1 Corinthians 10:13 NAS

Through each and every gray day, Mom was teaching me how a Christian faces the discouragement and disappointment of suffering. She had three ways of escape she skillfully used to endure. Sure, there were days when she was discouraged and blue, but they were scattered among the vast majority of sunny days, filled with smiles and laughter.

First, she had faith that God knew her and knew what was best for her. It was a simple, childlike faith that held no room for doubts and questions. It didn't matter if I understood; it didn't matter if the doctor was aware. It was enough that the Lord knew exactly how she felt.

"God knows, Julie," she said one day when I was troubled over someone who had hurt me. "Tell the Lord how you feel and then forget it. God knows, and He experienced the same kind of hurt. There is nothing I go through, but my Saviour had it much worse!"

Let us therefore come boldly unto the throne of grace, that we may obtain mercy, and find grace to help in time of need.

Hebrews 4:16

Nights were always the most difficult, when the pain raged, relentless and intense. Those were the times when she talked to the Lord constantly. I remember coming down, morning after morning, and saying, "How was it last night, Mom?"

She'd look up at me with a smile and say, "Pretty bad, sweetheart, but I just talked to my blessed Saviour all through the night. I asked Him to help me hold out."

She trusted the Lord completely to know what was best. "Don't hurry God," she admonished me once while I was expressing impatience. "I can't understand why it's taking so long for me to get well, but I know He loves me, and you don't interpret God's love by time." So she quietly waited and trusted and endured.

The second way she handled her intense suffering was by acceptance.

"How are you doing today, Mom?"

"No use complaining, honey. I can't do anything about

it, so no use talking about it. Complaining only makes
the devil laugh."

Often I wouldn't know how she was suffering, because
she didn't like to talk about it.

"You really want to know how I feel?" she asked once.
"Well, I'm short of breath, and the pain in my pelvis is
terrible. My stomach is sore, and there is a shooting pain
in my left arm. My hands feel tight and tingle in a most
irritating way. My right leg has a dull ache, and the heel
on the left foot and the right big and little toes throb
something awful. Plus, I can't see! Now do you see why I
don't talk about it? There's just too much to mention."

She never got hung up on why she was called on to
suffer so. "I've thought and thought and talked with the
Lord about everything I can think of that He might be
displeased with in my life, and as far as I know, everything is straight. So if there's something else, and that's
why I'm not getting well, then I'm willing for Him to
show me."

Her sickness certainly brought glory to God. People
wrote from all over the world, marveling at her ability to
sing for the Lord while undergoing such physical strain.

The third and most dramatic way she escaped her suffering was by meeting it with her great sense of humor.
"Might as well laugh about it, or I'll cry. If I didn't laugh,
the devil would have me in an insane asylum," she
would say.

She hated her looks in her thick glasses, and so she
joked about how they improved her looks. She was always so proud of her hair—long, beautiful, and thick—so
when the radiation treatments made most of it fall out,

she announced to me, "I asked the nurse to chop off all my hair. How do you like the effect of my short coiffure?"

As to how she handled old age, she often said, "I'm not too old to cut the mustard! I don't believe I'll ever think old. I'll always be able to laugh!" There was also no end of jokes about her weight and the inevitable slowness of her getting around. "I know why fat people are so good-natured," she would quip. "They have to be—they can't run!"

I learned to laugh with her when, because of her eyesight, she missed the glass while pouring water. I learned to chuckle with her about how her shoes had shrunk when her feet were too swollen to fit in them for a trip to the doctor. She taught me that to laugh is better than to cry.

One day she looked at herself in the mirror and smoothed down her dress, saying, "I shall be the handsomest corpse. I shall lie in my casket and just *scintillate!*"

She always had a comment about our clothes, or a nickname to kid us with. Even though the day would be difficult, Mom was there to cheer us up, to make us laugh. She showed me that there is a better way to live than by complaining, that I can trust that my Saviour knows, that I can accept courageously what He sends, and that I can always laugh at myself.

9

"I'm Not Afraid!"

Deep river,
My home is over Jordan.
Deep river,
Lord, I want to cross over
    into campground.
Don't you want to go
To that Gospel feast?
That promised land
Where all is peace?
Deep river,
I want to cross over into
    campground!
TRADITIONAL SPIRITUAL

Dawn was fast approaching, and my thoughts turned to plans of the coming day. I had scheduled a practical nurse to come over for a few hours, since I had promised to take our daughter shopping for school clothes. I would have to cancel the nurse first thing, before she started traveling here. Mom was too critical for me to leave this morning.

I thought perhaps I should call the doctor and take

Mom to the hospital in the morning. I didn't want to upset her, but possibly something more could be done to ease the agony she was going through. Or would it just prolong it? I remembered that we had discussed her condition a week before, when she took a turn for the worse. I reported to her that the doctor said he couldn't do anything more to ease her breathing unless she was admitted to the hospital.

"It's not that I'm being bullheaded and saying I won't go," she said seriously. "I don't ever want to talk to my Lord that way. But I've been there before, and it hasn't helped that much. Do you think it will help this time?"

It was a question I dreaded, but I didn't have to answer, because she went on to another more alarming one.

"I want you to be honest with me, Julie. How serious is my condition? What's different now that I didn't have before?" Then, throwing up her hands as if frustrated by trying to form the question, she said, "What's going on?"

I began slowly, choosing my words carefully, while at the same time breathing a silent prayer that the Lord would give me the right words. I remembered well what I had been taught: Always be honest with your patient, but don't take away his hope!

"Well," I began, "what's going on is that your kidneys are continuing to shut down more and more. You know this started happening last month, and instead of functioning better, they are getting worse."

She nodded her head.

I continued, "That is why you feel so heavy all over,

because your body is swollen from retaining the fluid your kidneys are not taking care of. Now, to compound the problem, the diuretics you are taking no longer seem to be working. We've tried larger and larger doses, and they don't help."

"How serious is that?" she questioned, impatient that I was taking so long to get to the point.

"It's serious. It's very serious. You can't live without your kidneys working—or at least one of them."

"Darlin'," she began, and then hesitated until I turned my head and looked directly into her pleading eyes. "Please, I don't want to die in no hospital!"

"Oh, Mom, we don't know if the Lord is going to take you home now or not. Fixing up kidneys is nothing for Him. Maybe He will, and maybe He won't. But whatever, it's up to Him. Right?"

"Right. It's up to Him!" she said with a finality that told me "end of conversation."

That night, as I sat next to the bed and looked down at that stricken face, I remembered how I purposely did *not* promise her I wouldn't take her back to the hospital. I knew that with terminal kidney failure, often the patient lapses into a comatose state for hours, even days, before death. It would be difficult to care for her here at home if she were unconscious. A comatose patient has to be turned frequently, and I had already discovered I could no longer turn her by myself. I thought of my close friend Eleanore Schellenberger, who is a nurse and had offered to come and spend the night. She was sleeping upstairs, available to help if I needed her.

I hadn't disturbed Eleanore all night because Mom

could breathe easier lying on her back, with the head of the bed elevated slightly. I reached over and placed a small pillow under one side of her back to ease the constant pressure. It seemed to help, because the constant groaning changed to heavy breathing.

When she did not respond in any way to my touch, I decided to check her blood pressure. As I had feared, the pressure had dropped considerably. I checked her pulse and felt adrenaline shoot through my body. The pulse had changed drastically. It was very slow and very irregular. I knew instantly that the overload of fluid in her body was too much strain on an already weak heart. Her heart was failing.

It was frustrating for me to know that my patient had an alarming heart arrhythmia (irregularity) and yet not take immediate action. If I were in the hospital and my patient's heartbeat changed so alarmingly, I would reach for an intravenous cardiac drug and administer it, hoping to stimulate the weakening heart. But that night I could do nothing—I *should* do nothing.

I sat down and went over the alternatives, trying to remain calm. I strongly believe that when a patient has a terminal illness, he has every right to choose where and how he will die. I had witnessed so many instances where the choice was taken away from a patient by a grieving family or an overzealous member of the medical profession. Often we frantically try to keep people alive, even against their own wishes.

I looked down at Mom. What if she were in a hospital, connected to a heart monitor, and we did administer drugs, and her heart was strengthened enough to keep beating a while longer? What would that accomplish? Would that take care of the kidney failure? No, I knew it wouldn't.

But we could put her on a kidney dialysis machine and rid her body of the wastes and extra fluid that had over-loaded her heart. Then what about the breathing problem? That could be taken care of with a respirator, but the cancer, the gangrene, the phlebitis in her legs, and the blindness could not be helped so quickly.

I could easily picture what would be the result to my precious patient, because I had seen it happen over and over. I could see the respirator wheezing noisily, hooked up to a tube in her mouth, making it impossible for her to talk. I could see the tears running down her cheeks as she felt the frustration of not being able to yell, "Let me die!" The kidney dialysis machine would be standing off to one side, waiting for its turn to work every other day. I could see the bedsores caused by not being able to move easily, the tubing strung up above and under the bed, the continuous injections. I could hear her groaning day after day from the pain, knowing there was no hope and wanting to go to a far better life, but not being allowed to leave.

The picture was too real, and I wanted to cry out. Yes, she had the right to stay here, if that's what she wanted. Yes, I would honor her choice, the Lord giving me strength. I would also honor the other wish she ex-pressed to me before.

"Julie, don't let anyone hook me up to any machines! When the Lord is ready to take me, don't let *anyone* try to hold me back!"

Ethel Waters had known she was dying for several years. It was nothing new to her. Twenty years before, an alarmed doctor had informed her that she could go at any time, since her heart was overworked from all the extra weight she carried.

"I'm not afraid to die, honey. I'm kinda lookin' forward to it!" she said one day to cheer me up when I was concerned about her condition. "I know the Lord has His arms around this big fat sparrow, and I'm not going to die one split second before the time the Lord already knows I'm going!" So she shrugged off the danger and continued to actively serve Him with all of her might.

She refused to take a date for any singing engagement far in advance, saying, "Any time it can happen that I'm going to my real home. I'm not in on the Lord's secrets, so I don't know when it will be."

Death is man's curse or his glory, depending on how he chooses to handle it. Ethel Waters chose it to be her glory, and in doing that, she taught me how a Christian faces death.

To her, death was both a friend and an enemy. She knew that God never intended that we should die. Death is the result of sin coming into the world. Although she had no strong fear of death, there was always the dread of facing an unknown experience. She had a strong natural desire to live and to fight off death as long as possible. Death would separate her from loved ones and take her to a place she had never been, even though she antici- pated what it would be like.

We didn't talk much about dying during the months Mom lived with us. She wasn't concerned with it. She

had already been given dying grace by her Saviour—
something we receive only at the time we need it.

We talked only of living the life now and the life to
come with her Lord. Death was a fact. She accepted it
and she trusted God to see her through it. She had lived a
full, exciting life, and she was ready to go. Her only
desire was to go while here with us and not in a hospital.

A few people were shocked at the fact that we were
letting someone die in a home with children. We didn't
feel that way at all. "Don't let her die in your home,"
they said with well-meaning concern. "The children
will be frightened."

It has only been during the last two generations that
we have tried to protect our children from death. But
children need to be taught that death is a fact of life, and
by seeing it in their own home, they can face it without
fear.

Our children were well prepared to accept their
Grandma Waters' death. They had heard her cries of
pain many times, and they knew she was going to God's
house, to a place already prepared for her. We had
prayed every day that God would take her home to His
house soon. When that day would come, they would
react with the joy of knowing that God had at last granted
our prayers and said, "Yes, she can come home now."

We explained that when this happened, her body
would "go to sleep" and she would look just like she was
sleeping, but she would already be in heaven with Jesus.
It is healthier to expose children to death in the right
way than to protect them from it.

There is nothing to fear from having a loved one die in

your home. Every day thousands of people die, and most of them are in institutions, away from family and friends. We need to put death in perspective and allow those who wish to stay in their own homes to do so.

For nine months I had been a witness to the testimony of how a Christian faces death. I watched the good days, when it all seemed distant, unreal. I watched the bad days, filled with discouragement, when it was obviously inevitable. There was no panic, no despair, no frantic search for escape—only acceptance, peace, and quiet confidence.

As I looked at her that night, so close to experiencing all of the wonders ahead, I was grateful for the opportunity of facing death with her.

10

Victory Over Death

When the trumpet of the Lord shall sound
    for me,
The glorious face of my dear Saviour
    I shall see.
I'll be with Him on that morning
    bright and fair.
'Cause when my name is called in glory,
Tell them I'll be up there!
Free from worry, free from pain,
Free from toil, and free from care!
TRADITIONAL SPIRITUAL

The murky darkness gradually lightened to a dark gray. The outline of the trees became barely visible through the loose-weave curtains drawn across the window.

I got up from the chair and opened the window just a little, letting in a breath of fresh, cool, early-morning air. The sweet smell of the gardenias blooming outside the window flowed in through the open crack. The birds were joining together, loudly heralding the beginning of a new day. Soon the sun would break through the moist, dewy fog, bringing another hot summer day.

I breathed a prayer of thanksgiving that the long night was over. Somehow, everything seemed better in the daylight, which helped to dispel the dark shadow of death. But no matter how ready we are for it, no matter how merciful it may be, we are seldom prepared to give up those we love.

I walked over to check my patient once again. She was quietly mumbling something over and over, as if talking to someone, but I couldn't understand what she said.

"Can you see something, Mom?" I asked as I leaned close to her. But the mumbling just kept on. I wasn't sure she had heard me.

The scene before me was now so pathetic I could hardly bear to look. Each slow breath was a desperate gasp, and I felt as if someone were choking me, too. She no longer responded to my touch or my voice in any way, but the groaning continued. Perhaps if I changed her position it would ease some pressure created by not moving all night. I quickly called Ellie, awakening her. I was grateful to have her with me those last minutes.

We discussed the pros and cons of moving her. Any nurse knows that when someone lies close to death, often turning the patient on his side is the final strain that brings the end. Yet it isn't good nursing care to let a critical patient lie motionless, either. We finally decided to move her.

We explained what we were going to do, but received no response. Carefully we repositioned her on her side and supported her with soft pillows. She responded only by muttering, "Merciful Father—precious Jesus."

Those were the last words she uttered. From then on there was only silence. I continuously held her wrist, feeling the pressure of her failing heart. I could sense its last struggle to keep beating. It had fought a losing battle for eighty years, and would not quit without a last final effort. The heartbeats were slow—much too slow to maintain life.

We sat down, one on each side of the bed, and waited in silence. By now the sun was bright, cars were racing by, and the floor overhead was creaking as my family began to stir. But nothing mattered. I sat tense and still, hanging on to every beat of the pulse I felt in my hand.

I had been taught that everyone knows when he or she is dying. I wondered if Mom was aware enough to know that she was about to take her final journey. I continued to talk to her softly, telling her how much she meant to me, to the whole family, and to her Saviour.

Suddenly the breathing changed to rapid, quick, shallow gasps, the groans became loud, and two small seizures racked her body. "Please, Lord," I pleaded. "No more. Please, please," I continued to plead.

I jumped up, wanting desperately to help. I was trained to help, but I knew there was nothing more I could do! Defeated and frustrated, I felt my tears begin to flow. Then I realized the Creator of the universe was by her side and in complete control. He wasn't wringing His hands in desperation. Why, then, should I?

My hand frantically searched up and down her wrists, but I could feel no pulse. One long desperate gasp came forth, then everything was quiet. Only the hiss of oxygen and quiet music from the radio interrupted the silence. They would no longer be needed. Life had gone on to a better place.

As her spirit moved on to its new home, the most wonderful look flowed across Mom's face. The lines of fatigue and weariness vanished, the strain of pain and suffering disappeared, and all I could see was *peace!* Ethel Waters had moved on. We were left with only an empty shell.

I buried my head in my hands as I sat down next to the bed. I could feel myself finally letting go of all the emotions held in so tightly for the past several months as I sobbed my heart out. But it was out of relief that I cried. The long night of suffering was over. She was on the other side, and I was left to remember. It no longer mattered to her, but the emotional strain had left its mark on those of us left behind.

Then, just as quickly as they came, the tears stopped and I stood beside her, looking down with love while tender thoughts crowded in. I wanted this time to myself—to thank God for answering our prayers, for the privilege of allowing Mom Waters to live and die in our home.

I took her hand and patted it gently. I felt no bitterness. How could anyone wish her back to such a body? If I resented anything, it was not being able to see what she was now seeing, to feel what she was now feeling, to live where she could now live forever, to see her meet her Saviour.

As I looked at her that moment, I pictured the lady who had once taken seventeen curtain calls for one per-

formance, now taking her last and final one to a standing
ovation as she entered heaven's gates. Only this time,
she joined in with the others, giving all the glory to the
One deserving it—Jesus Christ Himself.

For the last time, I kissed her forehead and said the
familiar "Good-night, sweet Mom. You are home now.
You are finally home!"

Finally Home

When surrounded by blackness of the darkest night,
Oh, how lonely death can be.
At the end of this long tunnel is a shining light,
For death is swallowed up in victory!

But just think of stepping on shore
And finding it heaven!
Of touching a hand
And finding it God's.
Of breathing new air,
And finding it celestial,
Of waking up in glory,
And finding it home!

DON WYRTZEN AND L. E. SINGER

11

Choose Now

Someday, you say, I will seek the Lord.
Someday I will make my choice.
Someday, you say, I will heed His word,
And answer the Spirit's voice.
Choose now, just now, while the Lord is here.
An angel your answer waits.
Choose now, just now, while the call is clear.
For tomorrow will be too late!

TRADITIONAL SPIRITUAL

As I mechanically moved through the day after Mom's home-going, doing the necessary things, I couldn't help but relive another September first—eleven years before. I had faced death suddenly on that day, as I heard the cold words on the telephone that my dear father had quickly been transported to his eternal home by a heart attack.

After the initial shock and denial were over, I found myself sitting on a plane, flying home and looking out the window at the beautiful white fluffy clouds. I recalled the many times my father had talked with joy of his "promotion day." But now I felt guilty because I didn't want to join in any celebration! I knew that one day we'd be reunited in heaven, but what about all the long days in the meantime?

I felt tricked, resentful, angry, and a hundred other emotions during the following days, as I numbly went about my duties. I knew 1 Thessalonians 5:18 so well: "In everything give thanks; for this is the will of God in Christ Jesus concerning you," haunted my rebellious spirit day and night.

In desperate need of comfort one day after my dad's death, I searched through one of his Bibles. In First Corinthians, the Lord provided what my soul longed for, as I read: ". . . Death is swallowed up in victory" (15:54).

It was nothing new; I had heard it all my life. But not until I needed the words for myself did the true meaning take its place in my heart—as the Holy Spirit of the Lord used the words to begin the healing process.

> O death, where is thy sting? O grave, where is thy victory? The sting of death is sin; and the strength of sin is the law. But thanks be to God, which giveth us the victory through our Lord Jesus Christ.
>
> 1 Corinthians 15:55–57

The first glimmer of silver lining began to show behind that dark cloud of grief as I read those words. I didn't have to go on being defeated by my sorrow. Death did not have the right to steal the joy of living. Jesus Christ had come to die so that I might have the victory over death. To sit and wallow in misery and self-pity was to make a mockery of His perfect costly sacrifice.

My eyes fell to the margin of my dad's Bible, where he had written his thoughts while meditating on this portion of Scripture.

O death, you cannot touch me! I will go to heaven without ever feeling your icy chill.

O grave, you had me (my body), but you could not keep me. My Lord has come and claimed me!

This is the triumphant shout of all who will go to heaven without dying.

For the first time I could "give thanks" honestly for what God had allowed. I could thank Him for putting me through some fire, to refine me and make me stronger. I could thank Him that the experience had drawn me closer to Him, causing me to love Him more and realize my need for Him more deeply. Yes, thank Him that from now on I would face life's inevitable trials a little wiser—with more resilience and a lot more maturity— and thank Him that without this experience I would never have been able to fully understand and help others who faced the pits of sorrow and grief.

Now, eleven years later to the day, I was meeting the death of a loved one again, but death had lost its grip on me. The truth of that lesson was still a part of me, and I could stand strong on the same promises from God in His Word.

Death is cruel and heartless, whether it comes suddenly or agonizingly slow. It comes to us as the punishment for sin, originally Adam and Eve's sin, and now our
own. We are born with a sinful nature, and therefore
born to face death one day as our penalty for sin. It's a
sobering thought, but something even more frightening
than physical death is spiritual death—being forever
separated from Almighty God.

But our Heavenly Father, in His infinite mercy, provided a way that we might have victory over death. He
sacrificed His own perfect Son, who bore our sins on the
cross, paying the price of our punishment, so that we
might go free. It was through this love gift that we may
have eternal life.

> For the wages of sin is death; but the gift of God is
> eternal life through Jesus Christ our Lord.
>
> Romans 6:23

Ethel Waters was prepared to die. She had accepted
this free gift and claimed Jesus Christ as her Lord
and Saviour. Because He conquered death and arose
from the grave, she had the assurance available to
all of us, that one day she too would live forever in His
heavenly home. If you have never received and
accepted this same gift, then you are not prepared to
die.

We all have to deal with death. We have to either
accept it as inevitable and prepare for it, or turn away in
denial, never making a decision as to the consequences.

Mom Waters loved to end her concerts with the song "Choose Now." She pleaded with her audience not to put off until tomorrow what could and should be taken care of today. We never know how many tomorrows we have left.

Neither was Ethel Waters afraid to die. She had confidence in the fact that she was prepared for death. If you are not prepared, then you should and will be afraid to die. There is a present-day popular movement which seeks blandly to take away all the fear of death. "Death is a peaceful passing on," it calmly states. "It is nothing to be feared, a mere biological process."

However, the Bible says, "And as it is appointed unto men once to die, but after this the judgment" (Hebrews 9:27).

To me, therein is a frightening thought. To face God's judgment without having previously accepted His Son is something I don't care to experience. You don't have to face that prospect either. You have been totally forgiven through the shed blood of Jesus Christ. It was complete forgiveness. There is nothing more you need to do but simply accept this free gift.

Having witnessed the deaths of many people, I realize that death can be a pit of darkness—or it can be a covered way which opens into light. We were given by our Creator the right to choose which way we will take.

To those of you who are already prepared to die, you need never be afraid. When we pass "through the valley of the shadow of death," our Saviour is there with us each step of the way, leading us out of the tunnel into the brilliant light of God's presence forevermore. Death cannot touch us; we have the victory through the death and resurrection of our Saviour Jesus Christ. We can go on with the joy of living!

> Because He lives . . . I can face tomorrow!
> Because He lives . . . all fear is gone!
> Because I know He holds the future.
> And life is worth living,
> *Just because He lives!*
>
> GLORIA AND WILLIAM J. GAITHER